Brimming with creative inspiration, how-to projects, and useful information to enrich your everyday life, Quarto Knows is a favorite destination for those pursuing their interests and passions. Visit our site and dig deeper with our books into your area of interest: Quarto Creates, Quarto Cooks, Quarto Homes, Quarto Lives, Quarto Drives, Quarto Explores, Quarto Gifts, or Quarto Kids.

This Edition Published in 2021 by Cool Springs Press, an imprint of The Quarto Group, 100 Cummings Center, Suite 265-D, Beverly, MA 01915, USA.
T (978) 282-9590 F (978) 283-2742 QuartoKnows.com

Cool Springs Press titles are also available at discount for retail, wholesale, promotional, and bulk purchase. For details, contact the Special Sales Manager by email at specialsales@quarto.com or by mail at The Quarto Group, Attn: Special Sales Manager, 100 Cummings Center, Suite 265-D, Beverly, MA 01915, USA.

25 24 23 22 21   1 2 3 4 5

ISBN: 978-0-7603-6857-2

Digital edition published in 2021
eISBN: 978-0-7603-6858-9

Library of Congress Cataloging-in-Publication Data available.

Design: Bad People Good Things
Photography: Chris Marshall

Printed in China

THE NEW 5-GALLON BUCKET BOOK

BUCKET BOOK

INGENIOUS DIY PROJECTS, HACKS, AND UPCYCLES

CHRIS
PETERSON

COOL
SPRINGS
PRESS

CONTENTS

INTRODUCTION

IT HAS BEEN SAID THAT "THE BEST THINGS IN LIFE ARE FREE." SO TRUE. FOR THE HOMEOWNER, THE HOMESTEADER, THE DIY'ER, AND THE CRAFTING CURIOUS, FREE IS ALWAYS THE PREFERRED PRICE. WHY PAY FOR SOMETHING WHEN YOU DON'T HAVE TO? UNFORTUNATELY HOME CENTERS AND HARDWARE STORES ARE STILL CHARGING VERY REAL PRICES FOR THE GOODS IN THEIR AISLES.

Take heart, though; there is an abundant do-it-yourself material that you can tap without ever taking out your wallet. That resource is the ubiquitous 5-gallon (18.9 L) bucket.

This humble container may not look like much, but it is amazingly adaptable and useful. Believe it or not, that rigid, round plastic form holds a potential air conditioner (page 12) to keep you cool in summer, a chicken feeder (page 77) to nourish your barnyard egg machines, and even a pitcher's helper (page 104) that can aid your future major leaguer in perfecting his or her split-finger fastball. It would be easier to list what you *couldn't* make with a 5-gallon bucket.

This new edition of the *5-Gallon Bucket Book* expands on the many projects of the first edition. You will still find incredibly useful standards like a **Portable Wine Rack** (page 37) so you never go thirsty at that outdoor Bach concert, and

handy **Sawhorses** (page 24) that ensure you have a no-fuss stable work surface nearby any time you need it. But now you can also enjoy the environmental and financial benefits of a **Rainwater Collector** (page 52), the luxury of a **Camp Shower** (page 58), or the pure gardener's delight of mounting an upcycled **Vertical Planter** (page 116) to take advantage or your precious little outdoor space. For this edition we've added more projects, more creativity, more useful tips, and more fun.

That's not to say you have to stick with the project designs in this book. They can just as easily be jumping-off points, inspiration for your own inner genius. There's no law that says you can't put your individual stamp on the 5-gallon bucket canon and create something truly unique. In fact that's a big part of this new edition: fun is a factor. Crafting 5-gallon bucket projects is just plain a blast. You don't risk a lot, because you won't be losing much if things don't come together the way you planned. And crafting something like an **Acoustic Speaker Dock** (page 107) can be as amusing as it is rewarding and useful.

Whether you're working off of one of the designs here, or going your own way with your own design, the tools and techniques you'll use are as basic as basic can get. A measuring tape, drill, jigsaw, and a little elbow grease are about all you'll need to get started. This edition expands on some of those basics, offering additional techniques within the new projects. But you probably know what you need to know—and own the tools you have to have—already.

Although this may not be a skill-building resource, the projects in the pages that follow could conceivably save you hundreds of dollars over the cost of store-bought versions. That's the real reward. Oh, and the pure satisfaction of making your own handy **Garden Cart** (page 125) or **Wall-Mounted Terrarium** (page 29) to delight and fascinate visitors to your home while amusing yourself.

You'll also be helping the environment because, for all their wonderful uses, 5-gallon buckets do not biodegrade. Far too many of them are cluttering landfills around the country. That's an especially egregious waste considering all the amazing creations they could become.

CHOOSING YOUR BUCKET

You won't have to look very long or hard to discover that not all 5-gallon buckets are alike. The vast majority—but certainly not all of them—are made of high-density polyethylene (HDPE). This plastic holds up well under high temperatures and releases low levels of contaminants. Low-density polyethylene containers are flimsier and will not tolerate higher temperatures or high-temperature contents. All the projects in this book should be executed using HDPE buckets.

Many of these projects, and probably many that you can create out of your own imagination, involve consumables of one form or another. The plastic in a bucket that will carry food or drink must be food grade. Non-food-grade plastic buckets may contain harmful compounds that can leach out of the plastic and into whatever's kept in the bucket—especially if any foodstuff you introduce is acidic. This is very important to keep in mind for projects such as the **Water Filter** (page 68).

If you're unsure of what the bucket contained before you got ahold of it, the bucket itself can probably tell you a lot about the original contents. Obviously, a label listing food contents such as beans, frosting, or salad dressing indicates food-safe plastic. Symbols on the label also offer clues. A snowflake means that the bucket (and its original contents) can be refrigerated or frozen. A wave symbol or dishes in water mean "microwave safe" and "dishwasher safe," respectively—all signs that the bucket contained food. The manufacturer listed on any label may be a giveaway as well. Do a web search for the manufacturer's name or any code on the bucket and you'll likely turn up what that manufacturer produces and puts into its buckets.

Lastly you can look on the bottom in the recycling triangle that is stamped on most buckets. A 1, 2, 4, or 5 inside that triangle tells you that the plastic out of which the bucket has been manufactured is safe for food. In most cases, a 7 and the term "bioplastic" means the bucket is food safe as well.

THE BUCKET BARGAIN

The best price for anything is free. Finding free five-gallon buckets is easy when you consider the many ways this exceptional resource is used. The trick is to hit up businesses that receive raw materials in the buckets but then have no reason to keep them.

RESTAURANTS, BAKERIES, AND OTHER FOOD RETAILERS. Any buckets you recover from these institutions are going to be food grade and are ideal for use in consumable projects. Of course, these buckets are also great for other projects. Make sure you clean the buckets thoroughly though.

BUILDING CONTRACTORS. Large renovation and building contractors often tear through five-gallon buckets of wall compound and regularly toss them right into an on-site dumpster. You'll need to thoroughly clean these buckets before use, but they are some of the tougher buckets you'll find. However, do not go onto a construction or private job site without permission. If the dumpster is on public property waiting to be emptied, it's fair game. That said, it's always nice to ask before taking.

SUPERMARKETS. Grocery stores order many different materials that are delivered in five-gallon buckets. Check the information under Choosing Your Bucket on page 7 to determine if buckets scavenged from a supermarket are food safe. You'll usually find the free buckets stacked near a dumpster. Some supermarkets recycle their plastic buckets, so, as always, it's a good idea to seek out the store manager and ask if the buckets are there for the taking.

SCHOOLS. Public school cafeterias and janitorial departments order both edibles and cleaning products in five-gallon buckets. Look for identifying labels and never assume a bucket rescued from a school dumpster is food safe.

CAR WASHES AND GAS STATIONS. Everything from industrial soap to grease can be delivered in five-gallon buckets, and most operations are happy to have the buckets removed. Here again, ask the manager or owner if it's okay to take the buckets.

Sometimes picking up a perfectly usable five-gallon bucket is just a matter of keeping your eyes peeled. Depending on how sophisticated your local recycling program is, the sanitation department or municipal dump may have buckets on hand that they would be more than happy to see reused. Often it's just a matter of asking the right person the right questions!

CHAPTER 1 AROUND THE HOUSE

SOME OF THE MOST USEFUL 5-GALLON BUCKET UPCYCLING PROJECTS ARE THINGS MADE FOR THE HOME. THIS CHAPTER INCLUDES USEFUL CREATIONS THAT CAN SERVE ANY HOMEOWNER WELL, INSIDE AND OUTSIDE OF THE HOUSE. THE GENERAL PROJECTS CAN FURTHER BE BROKEN DOWN INTO THOSE THAT HELP YOU WORK *ON* THE HOUSE AND THOSE THAT MAKE LIVING *IN* THE HOUSE A LITTLE BIT MORE COMFORTABLE OR EFFICIENT. AS A DIY'ER, YOU KNOW THAT BOTH ARE IMPORTANT.

In either case, most of these projects represent handy-dandy alternatives to units that would otherwise set you back a pretty penny. Economy coupled with efficiency is the hallmark of 5-gallon bucket creations, after all. Something like a **Small-Room Air Conditioner** (page 12) is not cheap, but the 5-gallon bucket version is amazingly inexpensive. And it works almost as well (plus, friends and family will be amazed at your ingenuity).

Many of these, such as the **Portable Wine Rack** (page 37), exploit the extremely durable nature of 5-gallon buckets. One of their most attractive features is the structural stability—and the fact that material itself holds up to wear and tear remarkably well.

But the real bonus is how easy these projects are to make. Even the most difficult one you'll encounter won't overly challenge a home DIY'er. That means frustration isn't a part of the process but a huge amount of satisfaction is!

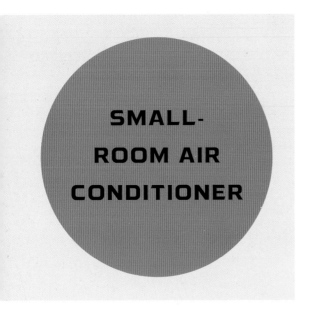

SMALL-ROOM AIR CONDITIONER

Even small window air conditioners can be mighty tough on the wallet. They aren't exactly packed with environmental friendliness either. The answer, as always, lies in a five-gallon bucket. Turn this simple container into a basic room-cooling unit that draws warm air in and blows cold air out. You can use this innovative bucket adaptation in any small space to chill a room for the price of a couple iced coffees.

Even though it does the job of a complicated air-conditioning unit, it does it in a simple way. The trick is to use the basic heat transfer physics of ice to your advantage. Instead of an energy-sucking compressor, the unit uses a basic desk fan. The fan draws warm air into the bucket, ice in the unit grabs ahold of the heat and gives off cold, and cold air is forced out of the PVC outlets. Easy peasy, all thanks to basic science.

Once you've built your own air conditioner, you'll want to ensure that it cools your space as effectively as possible. That means positioning the unit where it will have the greatest impact. Keep in mind that cool air is heavier than warm air and will tend to fall, while warm air rises. That means that the best location for a unit like this is up high. You can put it on a shelf, desk, table, or stepladder. Just make sure it's secure and stable. Orient the air conditioner so that the outlets blow wherever you want the air. You should also keep the unit out of direct sunlight, to prevent the ice from melting quicker than it normally would. Under average conditions, with the inside cavity filled with 1 to 2 gallons of ice, you can expect the unit to cool for 4 to 5 hours.

WHAT YOU'LL NEED

TOOLS:

Permanent marker, such as a Sharpie

Cordless drill and bits

1⅞" (47 mm) hole saw

Jigsaw or hacksaw

Keyhole saw

MATERIALS:

5-gal. bucket with plain lid

1½" PVC pipe, Schedule 40
(12" [30.5 cm] section)

80-grit sandpaper

Styrofoam 5-gal. companion liner

PVC pipe cement

Small plastic table fan (with cage lip
and a base that can be detached)

Silicone sealant

1-gal. resealable plastic freezer bags

Bags of dried beans (or other weight)

Time	Difficulty	Expense
45 minutes	Moderate	$$

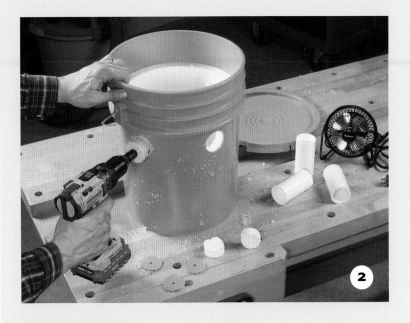

HOW YOU MAKE IT

1. Mark 3 holes about 5" down from the top of the bucket (or just below the lowest ridge on the bucket—below the mounting blocks for the handle). Use the end of the outlet PVC pipe as a template to trace the holes, tracing around it with the marker. Drill holes at the marked locations using the hole saw. Use sandpaper to smooth the edges of the holes, and then dry fit the pipe to ensure it fits snugly in the holes.

2. Slip the Styrofoam liner into the bucket and make sure it is secured all the way down inside (the liner can be somewhat flimsy, so don't let it flex inward during fabrication). Hold the liner tightly in place, keeping your hands and fingers safely away from the locations of the vent holes. Use the hole saw to drill through the three holes in the bucket to cut corresponding holes in the liner.

3. Cut the PVC pipe into three 4" sections using the jigsaw or hacksaw. Dry fit the pipe sections into the holes you've drilled in the bucket. Adjust the fit as necessary, and then apply PVC cement around the outside of each section, along the edge that will be inserted into the bucket. Slide the first pipe into place, so that only about ¼" of the pipe projects into the bucket through the Styrofoam liner. Repeat with the remaining pipe sections and let them dry.

4. Remove any stand or bracket from the fan. Center the fan body, face-down, on top of the bucket's lid. Use the marker to trace around the outside diameter of the fan's screen flange. Remove the fan and measure the width of the flange. Mark a second circle, inside the first, representing the inside diameter of the fan's flange (the fan will rest on its flange, when in place over the hole in the lid).

5. Drill an access hole and cut along the inside marked circle with a hacksaw or keyhole saw (A). Work slowly and try to follow the marked circle as closely as possible. Dry fit the fan into the hole, and make adjustments as necessary (B). Once the fit is snug, lay a bead of silicone sealant along the front of the fan flange and press it into place on the lid. Apply a weight, such as a few bags of dried beans, on top of the fan to press it against the lid until the sealant sets.

6. Fill 2 or 3 freezer bags with water and freeze them. (You can place them in a small pail or other mold to create a shape that will fit best into the bucket.) Once the bags are frozen, place them inside the bucket, making sure that none of the vent holes are blocked. Snap the lid onto the bucket, checking that the seal is tight all the way around the lid.

7. Plug in the fan and test the unit. Find the ideal location for the air conditioner, and orient the unit so that the outlets provide a stream of cool air exactly where you need it most. It's a good idea to time how long the air conditioner cools before the ice melts. You can then set a simple timer to alert you when the ice needs to be changed.

There are a number of alternatives to the materials used in this project. Adapt the basic idea here to what you have on hand, recycled materials, or what you can purchase at the lowest cost locally.

● **INSULATION.** If you can't find the Styrofoam liner used in this project (sold through home improvement stores as a "companion cooler"), you can line the bucket with double-sided roll insulation, strips of Styrofoam board insulation, or another insulating product (you can even cut down a beat-up Styrofoam cooler and use the pieces for insulation). The whole idea is to slow the conduction of the cold inside the bucket—and the heat outside of it—through the sides. The colder the inside of the bucket is kept, the slower the ice melts. For the same reason, no matter what material you use, you'll want to be sure to insulate the bottom of the bucket as well as the sides.

● **FAN.** The fan used in this project is an inexpensive desk fan, originally mounted in a stand with a U-shaped bracket. The construction is simple and easy to disassemble. You can use any small fan, as long as the motor is integral (completely inside or part of the wire cage surrounding the blades), and there is a flange of some sort to allow mounting. Although you can use a metal fan, this project uses a plastic one because not only is it cheaper, but the bond between the fan flange

and the bucket lid is extremely solid with silicone sealant. If you use metal or another material, you may need to use a different adhesive. You can also consider a USB fan if you'd prefer to power the unit through a computer's USB port. For safety be sure the fan is UL or CE approved.

● **OUTLETS.** The straight outlets in this project can be easily changed to direct cool air upward or off to the side (shown above). All it takes is a PVC plumbing elbow in a mating size to the 1½" PVC pipe. Attach the elbow with PVC cement. If you want to try out a direction, duct tape the elbow in place and use the cement only when you're sure the elbow is blowing air exactly where you want it.

● **ICE.** The core of this unit is ice. Capturing the ice in a separate container, such as resealable bags, saves cleanup time and makes filling or emptying the unit easy. However, you don't have to use the bags specified for the project. Although they are handy because you can freeze them in any shape that works for your bucket, you can also use plastic milk jugs, plastic liter bottles, or another plastic container that you want to recycle. The trick is to fill the interior of the bucket with as much ice as possible without blocking the outlets. The more ice, the longer the cooling will last without a refill.

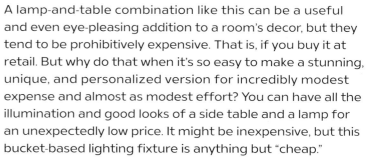

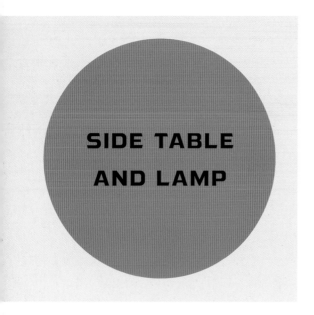

SIDE TABLE AND LAMP

A lamp-and-table combination like this can be a useful and even eye-pleasing addition to a room's decor, but they tend to be prohibitively expensive. That is, if you buy it at retail. But why do that when it's so easy to make a stunning, unique, and personalized version for incredibly modest expense and almost as modest effort? You can have all the illumination and good looks of a side table and a lamp for an unexpectedly low price. It might be inexpensive, but this bucket-based lighting fixture is anything but "cheap."

This one-of-a-kind piece of furniture is built from two buckets and ¾" PVC pipe and fittings. If you've done a little home renovation that involved plumbing, you might have everything you need just lying around. Even if you haven't, these materials are available for a song from the local home center. You'll find the lamp kit as well at stores large and small.

The construction is simple, even for someone who hasn't had a lot of experience with electrical wiring or circuits. The instructions for wiring the lamp socket to the cord come with the lamp kit and are as simple as simple can be. Essentially this will involve routing the cord up through the various pieces you use, tying a knot in the two wires, and screwing the exposed wires to the appropriate screws on the light socket. Easy peasy!

The bigger challenge is choosing the look you want, one that complements your interior design. You'll find a couple of options in the steps that follow, but they can be departure points for your own creative ideas. One of the wonderful things about 5-gallon buckets and PVC pipe is that they take paint so well. Use colored buckets or get your hands on a little plastic spray paint and some painter's tape, and the color schemes, patterns, or textures are all up to you. However, it's wisest to leave the shade itself white to maximize the amount of light that's transmitted.

WHAT YOU'LL NEED

TOOLS:

Measuring tape

Miter saw or table saw

Handsaw or jigsaw

Power drill and bits

Vise

Permanent marker, such as a Sharpie

Spade bit set

Frameless hacksaw or keyhole saw (optional)

MATERIALS:

¾" × 15½" (39.4 cm) PVC pipe (Schedule 40)

(2) 5-gal. buckets

80-grit sandpaper

¾" PVC cap (Schedule 40)

¾" PVC plug (Schedule 40)

Lamp kit with 10" (25.4 cm) to 8" (20.3 cm) harp, hardware, and 10' (3 m) cord

Plastic paint (optional)

PVC primer and cement

¾" PVC coupling (Schedule 40)

60-watt LED equivalent

Time	Difficulty	Expense
60 minutes	Moderate	$

HOW YOU MAKE IT

1. Measure and cut the ¾" pipe to length with a miter saw or table saw. Use a handsaw to cut around the bottom flange of the mouth of one bucket, using the flange as a guide. This will be the shade, so cut as carefully as possible. As an alternative, drill an access hole under the flange for a jigsaw and cut around the flange as cleanly as possibly using a fine-tooth blade. Clean up the cut edge with 80-grit sandpaper as necessary.

2. Drill ½" (13 mm) holes in both the PVC cap and the PVC plug (clamp each in a vise when drilling). The cap's hole should allow for the lamp kit ⅜" nipple to pass through without binding. If it doesn't, widen the hole slightly until it does.

3. Use the PVC plug inlet side as a template to mark the bottom of the base bucket with the marker. The plug hole should be centered on the bucket's bottom. Use the closest size spade bit to drill the hole out. *Note: Doing this from the inside over a sacrificial piece will guarantee against any cracking.* As an alternative, you can cut out the circle with a frameless hacksaw or keyhole saw.

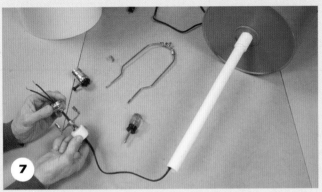

4. Use a spade bit to drill a ¼" (6 mm) hole in the side of the base bucket, right below the bottom ridge around the mouth of the bucket. Use the top nipple of the lamp harp as a template to mark a hole on the center of the shade bucket's bottom (the hole is usually ½" [13 mm], but check the harp you're using).

Optional: This is the best time to paint the pieces of the lamp table if you are going to finish them. Use plastic paint and let it dry completely before continuing. You can also decorate the shade bucket, now or later, by drilling a random pattern of very small holes all around the surface of the bucket. *Note: Where the pipe needs to be cemented into slip fittings, you'll need to rough up a painted surface with sandpaper before cementing them together.*

5. Prime and cement the plug into the coupling, with the plug on the inside of the base bucket, projecting up through hole in the bottom. Make sure the fit is as tight as possible and leave the connection to cure.

6. Run the cord end through the hole you drilled in the cap and then through the locknut and ¼" nipple for the lamp. Run the end up through the PVC pipe post. Cement the post into the coupling.

7. Run the cord end through the locknut and ¼" nipple for the lamp, and then through the hole you drilled in the cap. Pull the cord wires through the harp's base flange hole and slide the flange over the exposed end of the nipple. Screw the locknut onto the bottom of the nipple inside the cap, leaving about ½" (13 mm) of nipple on the other side. Pull the cord end through the light socket base, and then screw the base onto the exposed end of the nipple. Secure the nut inside the cap and the socket base so that they are hand tight.

8. Tie an underwriter's knot in the two wires at the end of the cord inside the socket base. Cement the cap onto the end of the pipe post. Follow the lamp kit package instructions to assemble the light socket.

9. Screw in a lightbulb and plug in the lamp to test that it works. Screw the shade onto the top of the harp and position the lamp next to a chair where it will be handy.

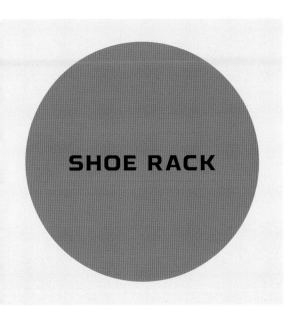

SHOE RACK

These days, "no shoes in the house" has become a common rule in a great many homes. Not only does a shoeless interior mean less dirt, mud, and muck tracked across carpets and wood floors, it's also a matter of home hygiene. Studies show that removing shoes can improve indoor air quality by keeping allergens and other particulates out of rugs and carpets, where they might otherwise exacerbate allergies, asthma, and related conditions.

If you're going to follow the trend, you'll need a handy place for shoes right by the entryway. Because they are often the most common entrance, mudrooms or informal side or back entrances often see more foot traffic (and dirtier gardening footwear). That's where this heavy-duty rack comes in. Positioned by a mudroom door, or under any entryway bench, it provides a convenient place to keep shoes and boots.

The truth is, this home accessory is more function than form—it's probably not attractive enough to sit in a well-appointed entryway or formal foyer. But it really comes into its own in a high-traffic area inside a busy back door.

With an open-weave metal top surface, this rack is ideally suited to sit on top of a plastic tray or other portable, waterproof, and washable surface. A tray meant for underneath a dish-draining rack can be an excellent option, as can a large sheet pan that is too battered for kitchen duty. The rack itself is easily cleaned whenever it becomes too dirty. Just drag it outside and give a good blast with the hose. Let it dry and it will be good as new. You can also spruce it up by painting the bucket a handsome color, and you can even paint the steel top surface a contrasting color. Or paint the whole rack bright white or black to blend right in with your mudroom decor.

Whatever the look, this will serve as perhaps the most durable shoe rack you've ever had. As a bonus, it's super easy to fabricate and assemble, needing no fasteners or modifications other than cutting. To make things even easier, the instructions here include different methods for making the cuts. Choose whichever suits the tools you have or the technique with which you're more comfortable.

WHAT YOU'LL NEED

	Time	Difficulty	Expense
	60 minutes	Moderate	$

TOOLS:

Ratcheting tie-down strap
Permanent marker, such as a Sharpie
Measuring tape
Straightedge
Cordless drill and bits

Jigsaw
Metal-cutting jigsaw blade
C-clamps
Hot glue gun and glue
Hacksaw (optional)
Cordless angle grinder (optional)

MATERIALS:

5-gal. bucket with lid
60-grit sandpaper
24×12×¼" expanded-metal sheet

HOW YOU MAKE IT

1. Fasten the lid on the bucket, and lay the bucket on its side on a work surface. Secure it with tie-down strap to keep it stable.

2. Draw a cut line straight across the center of the bottom, parallel to the work surface. Draw another line, parallel to, and approximately 3½" down from, the top line. This will be the bottom edge of the shoe rack.

3. Measure the distance from the point where the bucket contacts the work surface up to the bottom line. Mark this measurement on the lid, and draw a bottom cut line on the lid. Measure up from this line 3½". Draw a top cut line parallel to the bottom line.

4. Use the straightedge to extend top and bottom cut lines along the bucket's sides.

5. Drill a pilot hole on the top cut line. Use this to start the jigsaw cut. Repeat with the bottom line, sawing along the sides and finishing with

the lid. Make the cuts with a hacksaw if you have problems sawing through the lid with the jigsaw. Sand all the cut lines smooth.

6. Measure the dimensions of the cut bucket top opening (the width will be slightly different end to end, due to the bucket's taper). Subtract ½" and use the marker to transfer these dimensions onto the expanded-metal sheet.

7. Clamp the expanded-metal sheet to a work surface with the edge sticking out so that the cut line is unobstructed. Cut along one marked line using the jigsaw with the metal-cutting blade or an angle grinder. Rotate the sheet and repeat for each of the remaining three lines.

8. Position the cut expanded-metal sheet over the top bucket opening and carefully press it down. Press the edges down evenly until the sheet is stuck in the opening. Dab hot glue at several of the contact points—the more, the better. Sand any high points on the bottom edge as needed to ensure the rack sits flat.

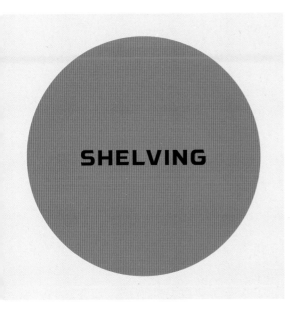

SHELVING

This much is true in a house, garage, and workshop alike: there is no such thing as too much storage. Shelving is some of the best storage because it allows you to keep everything organized in one easy-to-access place and in plain sight. Shelves are also space-efficient storage options. There are lots of shelving options, but a five-gallon bucket makes for a wonderful, self-contained shelving unit. Not only is a bucket the right size for a manageable shelf, but individual bucket shelves can be combined to create a shelf tower or even a wall of shelves as needed.

Turning buckets into shelves is a simple affair. The most challenging part of this particular project is cutting the plywood circle. Even though that shouldn't tax your skills, no matter what those skills may be, if it seems like a little bit more than you want to tackle, you can opt for the quick-and-simple solution of cutting a circle out of the bottom or lid of a sacrificial bucket. Cut the circle just a bit smaller than the top diameter and then push it down into the finished unit where the pressure of the sides with the lid on will keep the shelf in place (shave off the edges with a utility knife to make small adjustments). Just keep in mind that an unsecured plastic shelf won't support the heavy weight a screwed-in plywood shelf will. If you want to add stability, screw simple mounts to the inside of the bucket to hold the plastic circle in place.

The shelving can be used wherever there is a need, although it may not be entirely suitable for highly visible areas. Stack three of these units in a kitchen alcove for a handy pantry that is easy to clean. Or screw one to the wall in a mudroom for gloves and other foul-weather gear. The handle adds another dimension to this shelving unit. It allows the shelf to be hung from rafters in a garage or workshop, to keep tools and supplies at eye level, and makes it easy to move the unit at a whim. Just make sure your rafters can support the weight of whatever it is you want to store in the bucket.

TOOLS:

Permanent marker, such as a
Sharpie, or carpenter's pencil

Straightedge

Frameless hacksaw

Measuring tape

Carpenter's compass

Torpedo level

Cordless drill and bits

MATERIALS:

5-gal. bucket with lid

80-grit sandpaper

1" plywood scrap, at least 12×12"

(3) 1" Phillips roundhead wood screws

HOW YOU MAKE IT

1. With the lid removed, mark cut lines from top to bottom on the bucket, running up each side on the inside of the handle mounts so that the shelf opening takes up slightly less than half the diameter of the bucket. With the lid removed, use the straight-edge to mark the lines to points just above the bottom. Mark a horizontal line from the bottom of one vertical line to the other.

2. Use the hacksaw to make the cuts, starting at the top. Cut down one side, across the bottom, and up the other side. Sand the cut edges smooth.

3. Carefully measure the diameter of the bucket interior at the point where you want to position the shelf. Transfer this measurement to a small sheet of plywood, near one edge. Mark the center point. Position the compass point on the center point and draw a circle.

4. Cut in from the edge of the plywood with the jigsaw and carefully cut the circle out of the plywood sheet. Sand the edge smooth.

5. Position the shelf in the bucket (with bucket lid fastened on top). Use the torpedo level to ensure the shelf is level. Mark the outside of the bucket for the screws that will hold the shelf in place—one on either side and one on the back.

6. Drill pilot holes for the screws through the bucket and into the edge of the shelf. Secure the shelf with the roundhead screws.

A FIVE-GALLON SHELF TOWER OR WALL

Individual five-gallon-bucket shelving units can be combined to create columns or even whole walls of storage. The pattern of the shelving can be adapted to suit the space available, what you need to store, or your own preferences. No matter how you organize the shelves, you should follow some basic safety rules to ensure that they are as stable and secure as possible.

Stack columns of bucket shelves so that each successive bucket stands on the cover of the bucket below. The trick with this design is to ensure that buckets on top don't overload the lids on which they are standing. Store heavier materials on the bottom shelves, and position increasingly lighter materials as you fill the shelves above. Overall this is a good shelving structure when you need to organize and store lighter materials such as tubing, hoses, plastic fittings, or out-of-season clothing.

For a sturdier shelf structure—one that can support heavier materials on all the levels of shelves—create a running bond pattern stack. Center a bucket over where the two edges of the buckets below it meet. This creates a modified pyramid and ensures that the load is transferred from one bucket down through the sturdy walls of the buckets below it. In this formation, you can stack heavier items in upper shelves as well as lower shelves, and the shelving unit can in general support a lot more weight. This would be a good design for storing tools, gardening supplies, or family-size bags of food such as rice or flour.

Weight is just one issue. You also want to make sure that the shelving design you choose is stable. Regardless of whether you're building a shelving tower or a pyramid, screw the buckets in the second row and above to the wall. Either drive the screw directly into a stud or use a wall anchor. One screw per bucket should suffice. Lastly, to make the shelves more suitable for use in highly visible areas of the house, see **Painting Your Bucket**, below.

PAINTING YOUR BUCKET

It's easy to spruce up a five-gallon bucket project with some colorful paint. To ensure a lasting paint job, use a paint labeled for plastics, such as the Fusion for Plastic spray paint by Krylon (see Resources, page 142). In most cases, the paint will be a spray paint. Follow these steps to ensure success.

1. Set up your work area with proper ventilation, and lay plastic over anything you don't want painted. Wear proper safety gear, including a respirator rated for spray paints, safety glasses, and work clothes that cover most of your skin and your hair. Lastly, be sure you have enough paint on hand and 100-grit sandpaper. It also helps to have a solvent meant for use with aerosol paints, to clean up any mistakes.

2. Clean the bucket thoroughly and sand according to the paint manufacturer's instructions. Mask off any areas on the bucket you don't want painted.

3. Prime the bucket if necessary and paint according to the instructions on the can. To avoid drips, keep the spray tip in motion and lay down a very thin coat. You can always add a second coat.

RAINWATER COLLECTOR

Water is an increasingly scarce resource in many parts of the country—especially the West, where rules limiting watering the lawn and garden are common during the warmer seasons. In the face of potential droughts, the homeowner and home gardener are faced with letting their plants die due to lack of water. But it doesn't have to be that way.

A basic system to capture and store rainwater is easy to construct and trouble free to use. Although the system outlined in this project involves only two, you can set up a similar system with as many consecutive buckets as you need to make sure that you have enough water for your plants in drier times. The buckets are added in series, with the same plumbing connections used by the two here.

Optimizing that captured water is simple. You can use the attached spigot to fill a watering can, or just screw the end of a hose to the spigot. That way, you can direct the water you've saved exactly where it needs to go; gravity will do the rest.

Although this system features a sealed drain from the downspout into the first bucket, you can make things even easier for yourself by simply cutting the drain hole in the bucket's lid and rerouting the downspout directly into the hole. However, if you choose this shortcut, take measures to ensure that insects don't set up house in your buckets. You'll want to especially avoid letting mosquitoes breed by adding a little vegetable oil to the water in your buckets or using any of the many off-the-shelf solutions you'll find at local hardware stores or larger home centers.

WHAT YOU'LL NEED

TOOLS:

Permanent marker, such as a Sharpie

Cordless drill and bits

Jigsaw

¾" (19 mm) Forstner bit

C-clamps or hold-down strap

Channel-lock pliers

4" (1.2 m) carpenter's level

MATERIALS:

(2) 5-gal. buckets with lids

Plastic downspout extensions

Brass rain barrel spigot, washer,
and flange nut

½" PVC pipe

½" PVC threaded male adapter

½" PVC threaded female adapter

PVC primer and cement

½" rubber washers

(3) ½" PVC couplings
(or ½" plastic flange nuts)

Cinder blocks

Time	Difficulty	Expense
60 minutes	Easy	$$

HOW YOU MAKE IT

1. Use the outlet end of the downspout extension as a template to mark with the marker an opening in the top of one bucket's lid. Drill an access hole and cut out the opening with a jigsaw.

2. On one side of the bucket, just below the lowest rim flange, trace around the end of the ½" nipple to mark a hole. Use a ¾" (19 mm) Forstner bit to drill out the hole. Mark and drill a companion hole in the exact same place on the second bucket.

3. On the opposite side of the bucket, mark and drill an identical hole for the drain about 1" (2.5 cm) down from the top edge. This will most likely mean drilling between ridges on the top of the bucket. Take your time and hold the drill level as you penetrate the side of the bucket. It's best to use a helper to hold the bucket, or otherwise clamp or strap the bucket down to a work surface.

5

9

4. On the same side as the drain hole, use the threaded stem of the brass hose bib to mark a hole about $1/2$" (1.3 cm) up from the bottom of the bucket. Drill out the hole carefully so that you don't enlarge the hole. The fit should be tight.

5. Place the two buckets side by side so that the holes for the connecting pipe are facing each other. Screw a male adapter into the female adapter through one hole, with a washer between them on the inside of the bucket. Hand-tighten as much as possible, and then use channel-lock pliers to tighten the couplings or nuts a quarter turn more. Repeat with the opposite bucket. Use PVC primer and cement to adhere the tube into the male adapter on both sides

6. Repeat the process for the overflow tube at the top of the bucket.

7. Install the plastic hose bib in the bottom hole. Use a rubber washer on both inside and out.

8. Place cinder blocks where you want to locate the system (usually as close as possible to directly under the downspout). Level the ground under the blocks and ensure the blocks are level using a 4" (1.2 m) carpenter's level. Position the buckets on the cinder blocks.

9. Attach a flexible downspout extension to your rain gutter downspout. Secure the lids on both buckets; ensure that the first bucket's lid is positioned so that the downspout opening is opposite the second bucket. Slip the nozzle of the downspout extension into the hole in the lid.

PROJECT OPTIONS

Capturing rainwater can be an incredibly environmentally conscious way to keep your landscape hydrated. A system like the one in this project is an easy, low-cost, and low-maintenance way to do that; but it's also an adaptable construction. Add buckets in the line as your needs require and to take advantage of heavy seasonal rainfall when the rest of the time your local climate is fairly dry.

Using white buckets will limit evaporation, but you shouldn't feel constrained to do this. You can paint the buckets lighter or pastel colors and still enjoy the same effect. Two ounces (59 ml) of bleach added to each bucket during a rainy season will limit the growth of mold or algae, but give the water a month for the bleach to evaporate before using the water on plants— especially any edibles such as fruit trees or vegetables.

Regardless of whether you add bleach, you should clean the entire system a couple times a year to prevent the buckets from becoming overly attractive to mosquitoes and other critters and to keep the water flowing efficiently throughout the system.

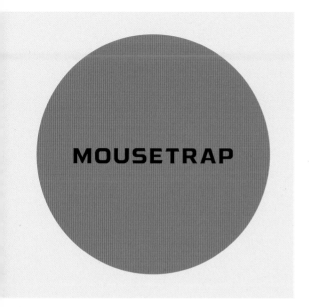

MOUSETRAP

Mice are bothersome pests that, left to their own devices, can multiply into a serious problem and even an infestation in short order. Not only do they eat or otherwise destroy food, they also contaminate food areas with feces and can even spread illness. They commonly gnaw through wiring and can create serious situations in walls that can be quite expensive to fix.

The secret to making sure a mice problem doesn't get out of hand is to deal with it quickly and completely. You can poison the little critters, but that can lead to as many problems as it solves (decomposing mice in the walls are not a smell anyone wants in their home). That means using the best mousetrap you can find—or in this case, make.

There are many different mousetrap designs on the market, all with their own pros and cons. But really, why not make your own, super-effective mousetrap? It's easy to do with a few implements you probably have lying around the house right now. This particular design is also fairly ingenious, and mice will usually not learn to avoid it, as they might with other traps.

The beauty of this design is that it can be used time and time again, unlike a glue trap. And unlike a snap trap or other kill traps, disposing of the mice is easy with a five-gallon-bucket trap; no need to touch the bodies at all! It will be up to you to decide whether you want to kill the mice or catch and release them. Catch and release is a much more humane method (take the mice at least a mile from your home before releasing them into a park or other semiwild area). If you opt to kill them, fill the bucket about one-quarter full with antifreeze; it will kill the pests quickly and will diminish any telltale odor.

Keep in mind that any mousetrap—this one included—needs to be positioned and baited correctly to be effective. Read the guidelines in **Keys to Capturing Mice**, page 28. You should also continue using the trap until you're absolutely certain that there are no mice left in the home.

TOOLS:

Cordless drill and bits

MATERIALS:

Permanent marker, such as a Sharpie, or pencil

¼" wood or steel dowel (at least 15" long)

5-gal. bucket

Scrap of 1" PVC pipe (6 to 8" long [15 to 20 cm])

1×3" (or similar) scrap, 15 to 18" long

Duct tape

HOW YOU MAKE IT

1. Lay the dowel across the top of bucket and mark the locations of the drill holes about 1" below the lid. Drill ¼" holes for the dowel on each side of the bucket at the marked locations.

2. Slide the dowel in through one hole. Slide the PVC scrap onto the dowel, and push the dowel out through the opposite hole. (You can use a soda can if you don't have a scrap piece of PVC pipe).

3. Duct tape one end of the 1×3" scrap to the lip of the bucket at one end of the dowel, resting the other end on the floor to create a ramp. Slide the PVC pipe section to the ramp end of the dowel and bait the top of the pipe with a generous dollop of peanut butter mixed with sunflower seeds; it should spin freely around the dowel to drop any mouse that tries to get at the food into the bucket. Position the trap where there is evidence of mice, and regularly check the trap. Rebait as necessary.

KEYS TO CAPTURING MICE

Reusable mousetraps are most effective when you position, bait, and maintain the trap carefully. Here are a few things to keep in mind:

● Position the trap where mice have been active in the last 24 hours. (Look for droppings, gnawed wiring or wall surfaces, or chewed food.)

● It's best to position the trap along a wall, away from foot traffic, and not in a corner. Try to establish the vermin's paths of travel (mice often scurry along a wall to get to one part of a room or another), and place the trap in a regularly used path.

● Bait the trap with peanut butter and birdseed to start with. If you're not successful, change the bait. Chocolate and bacon are popular baits as well.

● If you're not using antifreeze inside the bucket, check and empty the trap often or other mice will become wary of it.

WALL-MOUNTED TERRARIUM

WHAT YOU'LL NEED

TOOLS:

Permanent marker, such as a Sharpie

Handsaw and jigsaw

Paintbrush

Compass or trammel

Cordless drill and bits

Phillips head screwdriver and stud finder

MATERIALS:

5-gal. bucket (white)

100-grit sandpaper or acetone

Flat white paint for plastic

⅛" (3 mm) plexiglass

(6) 5 mm nylon shelf support pins

Silicone adhesive

(2) 2½" (6.4 cm) flathead wood screws and washers (and anchors, if needed)

Decorative rocks or pebbles

Air plants

Time	Difficulty	Expense
45 minutes	Moderate	$$$

Part of enjoying any home is decorating it with entirely unique features that catch and delight the eye. Few decorations fill the bill better than this wall-mounted stunner, a terrarium that floats on a vertical surface and invites people to peer inside.

This is a true conversation starter and will be even more impressive if it is partnered with two more. That's not a problem, because the terrarium is so easy to make and, once fabricated, requires virtually no maintenance (you'll be planting your terrarium with air plants—no soil or watering necessary).

This is yet another great project on which to include kids. Not only will they enjoy the interesting and unusual techniques used, but they will also see the potential in the terrarium—far beyond just plants. You can use colored marbles instead of rock, create a diorama scene with miniature figures such as those used on a miniature train setup, and even more. Maybe the kids want to paint the bottom of the bucket with a scene to create the illusion of a far-off world! It's a departure point for imagination and pure fun.

Fun should always be paired with safety, which is why you want to be careful to mount this creation securely. Because of the rocks, it can be heavy. If you are not driving the mounting screws into a stud, it's essential to use high-quality wall anchors to ensure the mount is completely secure.

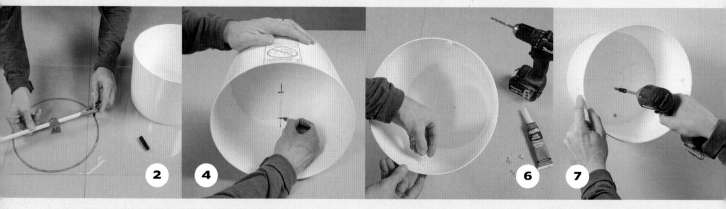

HOW YOU MAKE IT

1. Measure and mark a line all the way around the bucket, 8" (20.3 cm) up from the bottom. Use a handsaw to cut the bucket on the line. Discard the top section, and lightly sand the surface of the bucket to remove any marks and create a clean, matte surface (use a paintbrush to paint the bucket flat white if it has logos or other markings on it that you can't remove by sanding). As an alternative, you may be able to properly prepare the surface with acetone.

2. Use the mouth of the bucket as a template to mark a circle on a plexiglass sheet. Use a compass or trammel to mark a second circle inside the first. The second circle should be ¼" (0.6 cm) less in diameter than the first. Mark a center line through both circles.

3. Use a jigsaw to cut out the inner plexiglass circle, and cut it in half along the center line.

4. Measure and mark several screw locations on the inside bottom of the bucket. These should be spaced evenly across what will be the bottom half of the bucket when it is mounted. (The decorative stone and plants will hide the mounting screws.) Drill holes at the marks.

5. Position the plexiglass half circle into the mouth of the bucket and hold a nylon pin in place at one top edge. Mark the pin location and repeat the process with a pin on the opposite side of the window, and at the bottom, centered on the half circle. Mark pins at the same locations on the inside of the plexiglass window.

6. Remove the window and drill ⁷⁄₃₂" holes for the nylon pins (there is not a direct conversion from 5 mm to inches, so drill the holes with a ⁷⁄₃₂" bit and, if the pin won't fit, move up to a ¹⁵⁄₆₄" bit; the fit should be snug in any case). Coat the first inside pin post with silicone adhesive and place it in the hole. Repeat with the remaining two inside pins and let the adhesive dry before proceeding.

7. When the inner pins are set, mount the terrarium in the final location. Uising the stud finder, mark the wall for mounting through the predrilled mounting holes in the bottom of the bucket. For any holes that won't be drilled into a stud, install an appropriate wall anchor. Use a Phillips head screwdriver to screw the terrarium to the wall, using washers between the screwheads and bucket bottom.

8. Position the plexiglass window, and install the outer pins in the same way you did the inner pins. Let those pins set before proceeding.

9. Dab paint over any mounting screwheads that might be visible. Fill the bottom half of the terrarium with decorative rocks, and tuck in the air plants you've chosen.

HELPFUL HANDCART

	Time	Difficulty	Expense
WHAT YOU'LL NEED	20 minutes	Easy	$

TOOLS:

Measuring tape

Permanent marker, such as a Sharpie

Hacksaw

Level

Rasp file, rotary tool, or utility knife

Cordless drill and bits

Crescent wrench

MATERIALS:

(1) 1¼" × 40" (101.6 cm) PVC pipe for handle post (Schedule 40)

(2) 1¼" × 5" (12.7 cm) PVC pipe for handles (Schedule 40)

5-gal. bucket

1¼" (3.2 cm) steel pipe straps

PVC primer and cement

1¼" PVC tee (Schedule 40)

#10 ½" sheet metal screw

(4) ¼" × ¾" hex-head bolts and nuts

¼" washers

½" × 14" (35.6 cm) metal rod

(2) ⅝" washers

(2) 6" (15.2 cm) replacement wheels

(2) ⅝" hub push nuts

This tough little tote goes wherever the action is and can take a beating and then some. It's constructed nearly entirely of durable PVC plastic, with wheels that can plow forward even over rough surfaces.

The size of this carrier is just big enough to schlep a reasonable amount of materials or tools, but not so big as to be unwieldy. For more carrying capacity, consider the **Garden Cart** on page 125, which can be brought inside as necessary.

You have a lot of options to make this construction even more durable if you prefer. Swap out the PVC pipe handle for ¾" cast iron plumbing pipe to make the handle assembly entirely indestructible. Replace the 8" (20.3 cm) wheels with more rugged 10" (25.4 cm) or 12" (30.5 cm) replacement wheels (bigger wheels are often labeled "handcart replacement wheels") to create greater clearance to navigate obstacles. Of course, you can also make aesthetic adaptations. If you prefer to use this for lighter duty and want it to be more attractive, you can always paint the bucket and/or the handle assembly—or paint them contrasting colors for an eye-catching appeal.

HOW YOU MAKE IT

1. Measure, mark, and cut the 1¼" PVC pipe to the length listed on the materials list. Either have the home center or hardware store cut the axle to length, or cut it to length using a hacksaw.

2. Turn the bucket upside down and use a straightedge to make four compass marks equidistant around the bottom of the bucket. Make sure the marks extend over the bottom rim so that they can be seen from the sides.

3. Turn the bucket right side up and use one of the marks as a reference point for a level. Hold the level parallel to the length of the bucket and mark a line up from the reference mark to the lip of the bucket (it will be impossible to draw an unbroken line; draw as clearly as you can).

4. Use a rasp file, rotary tool, or—as a last resort—a utility knife to sand down the bucket flanges along the handle line and about 1" (2.5 cm) on either side. This must be done to ensure the handle sits flat to the side of the bucket.

5. At one of the marks 90 degrees from the mark you just made, measure 1" (2.5 cm) up from the bottom and mark for the axle hole. Repeat with the mark opposite the first hole. Drill out both holes with a ½" (13 mm) bit (wiggle the bit a little

to enlarge the holes slightly and allow the axle to freely slide through the bucket).

6. Hold the PVC pipe handle post in place aligned with the vertical line you marked. Dry fit a pipe strap on the handle about 3" (7.6 cm) up from the bottom. Mark the flange hole locations on the bucket. Remove the strap and pipe and drill ¼" (6 mm) holes at the marked strap location.

7. Use PVC primer and cement to fasten the PVC tee onto one end of the handle post. Cement a handle grip into each side of the tee. Let the PVC cement fully cure before continuing.

8. Drive a sheet metal screw through the bottom pipe straps into the handle post to secure it in place. Bolt it in place and then mark the location of the second, top strap, which should be about 3" (7.6 cm) down from the top.

9. Drill holes in the bucket for the second strap. Use ¼" washers between the bolt head and bucket, and nuts and bucket. Tighten the nuts with a crescent wrench.

10. Slide the metal axle through the holes in the bucket sides. Slide a washer and then a wheel on one end. Secure the wheel in place with a hub push nut. Repeat with the opposite wheel.

BIKE RACK

WHAT YOU'LL NEED

TOOLS:

Permanent marker, such as a Sharpie

Carpenter's level

Handsaw

Jigsaw

Measuring tape

Circular saw or table saw

Cordless drill and bits

MATERIALS:

5-gal. bucket with lid

2×4

(4) 6" Torx deck screws

(8) 1½" washer-head (pocket hole) screws

Painter's tape

120-grit sandpaper

Time	Difficulty	Expense
30 minutes	Moderate	$

This is one of those handy features few homeowners would think to buy themselves, much less make. But once you put a bike rack to work organizing your various two-wheel conveyances, you'll wonder how you ever could have done without it.

You have only to run the car over, trip over, or pick up fallen bikes a few times to appreciate what a simple, durable, and inexpensive bike rack brings to the table. Bikes are best kept upright and organized to avoid the worst kind of garage or front yard clutter. Not only are scattered bicycles unsightly and a hazard underfoot and undertire, lying them on the ground is a sure way for them to rust out or get damaged.

One of the best features about this particular bike rack is its durability. It will hold up to abuse and harsh weather and is just about impossible to destroy. It's also lightweight enough to be totally portable. It can go on a patio, be moved to the garage, and then do mountain bike duty in the back of a pickup. No sweat!

This rack holds one bike, so if you have a bigger bike-riding brood, make as many as you need. Adapt them to the size of bike tire (for instance, you can make the tire slots narrower if the bikes in your house are all kid-sized models). You can connect them for stability's sake by running a 12" (30.5 cm) leg in place of one 6" (15.2 cm) leg on one side of two racks. No matter what, they're inexpensive and easy to construct, won't take up a lot of room, and will last virtually forever.

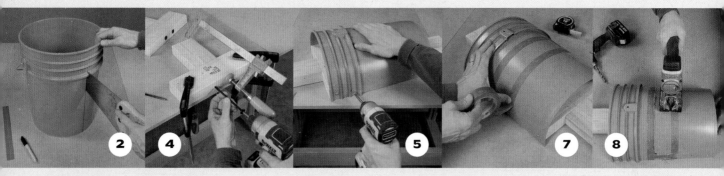

HOW YOU MAKE IT

1. Mark a center line across the top of the bucket with a marker, using a carpenter's level as a straightedge. Stand the bucket on a flat, level surface and use the carpenter's level to continue the lines down on each side. Turn the bucket upside down and continue the center line across the bottom.

2. Remove the lid and follow the cut lines to cut the bucket in half with a handsaw. You can also use a jigsaw, although it can present a challenge given the variations in thickness and shape along the cut line. Use the jigsaw to cut the remaining bottom off the bucket, following the bottom edge.

3. Lay one end of the bucket, cut side down, on a 2×4 and mark the board for brace cuts. Repeat with the opposite end. Measure and cut both 2×4 braces to size with a circular saw or table saw. Cut two 2×4 legs 6" (15.2 cm) long.

4. Measure and mark the center point along the length of each brace. Use the mark as a reference point to position a 6" (15.2 cm) leg perpendicular to each brace, forming a T. Drive 6" Torx deck screws through the opposite edge of each brace and into the end of each leg. Use two screws per brace.

5. Set the appropriate brace at one end, on the inside of the bucket with the leg positioned outward. Use 1½" washer-head (pocket hole) screws to screw the bucket to the ends of the brace. Repeat with the second brace at the opposite end of the bucket.

6. Measure and mark the center point along the length of the bucket half. Measure and make the same mark on either side of the bucket. Measure and make marks on either side of the center points; these represent the edges of the tire slot. The tire slot shown is for a standard adult ten-speed—the slot measures 2¼" (5.7 cm) wide. A mountain bike would require a slot 3¼" (8.3 cm) wide, although balloon tires might require a slot up to 4" (10.2 cm) wide. Size the slot according to the bike that will be used in the rack.

7. Use painter's tape to connect the outside marks and outline of the tire slot. The slot should terminate about 1½" (3.8 cm) from the bottom edge on both ends.

8. Cut out the tire slot. Drill an access hole inside the marked area and use a jigsaw to cut along the line. Use 120-grit sandpaper to smooth the cut edges.

Optional: Secure the bike stand on a dirt or grass surface by driving stakes and nailing them to the legs. You can stabilize the stand on a concrete surface or a wood deck by setting weights on the legs, such as bags of cement or empty paint cans filled with rocks or dirt (you can even nail the cans in place prior to filling them). It's also easy to accommodate several bikes with the same idea.

LONG-HANDLED TOOL HOLDER

WHAT YOU'LL NEED

TOOLS:

Measuring tape

Permanent marker, such as a Sharpie

Level

Circular saw or miter saw

Power drill and bits

V-block or vise

Side cutting pliers

MATERIALS:

5-gal. bucket

(4) 2" × 16" (40.6 cm) PVC pipe (Schedule 40)

PVC primer and cement

(4) 2" PVC caps (Schedule 40)

10" (25.4 cm) zip ties

Time	Difficulty	Expense
40 minutes	Easy	$

If you have ever experienced the particularly jolting surprise of stepping on the blade of a shovel or rake, only to have the handle fly up and nearly fracture your skull, you'll know how long-handled tools have a propensity to find their way underfoot. It's tremendously disconcerting but understandable. On any job site or project, there's rarely a good place to put long-handled tools.

What's more, lying around isn't good for the tools. It's too easy to leave them wallowing in destructive water, dirt, mud, or worse. Cars can back up over them; wheelbarrows can rumble on top of them. They really need to be kept out of the muck to extend their life spans and prevent accidents. That is, however, easier said than done.

Many homeowners have garage or storage shed solutions for storing all their long-handled tools. Racks or hangers are excellent for keeping these particular tools up off the floor and out of the way. The problem is, those storage solutions aren't portable. When it comes time to put the tools to use, you're left with carting heavy, unwieldy objects to wherever the work needs to be done and, once again, leaning them on the nearest vertical surface or resigning yourself to plopping them down on the ground.

This project answers both the transportation quandary and the issue of site-storage needs. The bucket will easily accommodate four tools around the outside and offers additional space in the actual bucket, where you can put smaller tools like hand trowels or material like loose topsoil. You can add tubes using the same method outlined, but be careful not to crowd the tools and keep in mind that the working ends of the handles usually take up more space than the handles themselves.

HOW YOU MAKE IT

1. Measure and mark four points equidistant around the top of the bucket. Use a level to mark straight lines down the side of the bucket at each of the points. Mark three horizontal lines around the body a couple inches in from each end and another centered along each line (roughly 1" [2.5 cm] above the cap; 8" [20.3 cm] up the pipe; and 4" [10.2 cm] down from the top).

2. Cut all the pipe sections with a circular saw or miter saw. Use the PVC primer and cement to adhere a PVC cap onto one end of each pipe section.

3. Mark hole locations 1" (2.5 cm) from either side of the vertical lines along the horizontal lines (these are zip tie access holes). Mark and draw layout lines on each pipe to match the horizontal lines when the pipes are in position. (Use a small piece of flexible cardboard to mark these lines.)

4. Repeat the process for all four pipes. Place a pipe in a V-block or vise and drill two ¼" (6 mm) holes, separated by 1" (2.5 cm), at the marks. Repeat for the remaining pipes. Drill ¼" (6 mm) holes at all the marks on the bucket.

5. Attach the pipes one at a time. Start by weaving the end of a zip tie through a bucket hole from the inside, then guide it in through a corresponding hole in a pipe, back out through the opposite pipe hole, and then in through the opposite bucket hole. Secure the zip tie and use the side-cutting pliers to clip the excess length off the zip ties.

6. Repeat the process with the remaining holes in the pipe, then repeat for the remaining three pipes.

PORTABLE WINE RACK

The easy-carry handle and impact-absorbing construction of a five-gallon bucket make for a perfect traveling wine rack that ensures four bottles of your favorite vino will arrive safe and sound, no matter where you're going or how rough things get on your way there. Of course, you might be the type of oenophile that prefers to keep your wine stash safe and sound at home. In that case, you can craft multiples of this rack and stack them to store your favorite vintages in the basement, garage, or other cool, dark place.

Foam insulation board in the bottom of the bucket protects the bottles in either case. Each bottle is given its own cozy PVC home. This ensures that the bottles don't smack against each other and provides ironclad protection against breakage. You can adapt the rack a bit to suit whatever wine you'll be storing. The four tubes here are meant to accommodate both standard 750-milliliter bottles and wider bottles of sparkling wine or champagne. If you want to dedicate the rack to just white or red, you can use 3½" PVC pipe instead of the 4" width specified here. That will allow you

to add a pipe and increase the capacity of the rack by one bottle. You may also want to customize your rack if you want to secure the lid on top during transport (the design below allows for the necks of the bottles to stick up above the top of the bucket, making it easy to grab them). If you do want to use a lid, you'll need to remove one layer of the bottom insulation board, so that the bottles sit lower and the top fits neatly over the rim of the bucket.

No matter what you're storing, though, if you're keeping the wine in the same place for longer than a week, store the rack on its side to ensure the wine corks don't dry out. Also keep the rack out of direct sunlight whenever possible. The sun's rays can degrade the wine. That's a good reason to paint the bucket—which is also your chance to decorate it so that it pleases the eye as much as the palette.

WHAT YOU'LL NEED

	Time	Difficulty	Expense
	30 minutes	Easy	$

TOOLS:

Table saw or hacksaw

Measuring tape

Permanent marker, such as a Sharpie

Utility knife

Mallet (optional, for tapping pipes down into the bucket)

MATERIALS:

4" PVC pipe (42" [106 cm] section)

5-gal. bucket

Sheet of 2" foam insulation board (2×2" or 4×8")

Expanding foam sealant

HOW YOU MAKE IT

1. Cut the PVC pipe into 4 pieces 10½" long. Use the bucket bottom as a template to outline 2 equal circles out of a sheet of foam insulation board. Cut the circles out with the utility knife, cutting slightly inside the marked line. Stack the board circles in the bottom of the bucket.

2. Push the pipe sections down into the bucket in a cloverleaf pattern. Because the bucket narrows toward the bottom, you may need to tap the pipe sections down. The top edges of the pipes should be even with the top edge of the bucket, and the bottoms of the pipe should be in contact with the top foam circle.

3. Spray the expanding foam sealant around the spaces between base of the pipes. Spray only a little at a time, allowing it to fully expand before spraying more and holding the pipes down in the bucket as necessary. Spray in enough sealant to fill about 2" of each space. Repeat with each cavity. The pressure created by the sealant between the pipes and the bucket surface will hold the pipes in place.

Alternative: If the pipes squeeze up before you can spray the cavities with the expanding foam, you'll need to secure them in place. To do this, secure the lid on the bucket over the pipes and drill 1" holes over the cavities between the pipes. Use the holes to spray the expanding foam sealant into the cavities between the pipes, working slowly and carefully.

VARIATION: **PORTABLE BEER COOLER AND STORAGE**

It's easy to adapt this project to beer bottles if your tastes tend more toward suds than wine. Because the diameter of a beer bottle is smaller than that of a wine bottle, you can fit more openings in this carrier than you would in a wine rack. Also, because you won't be storing the beer on its side, the cooler is crafted so that the tops of the bottles sit below the top edge of the bucket. This means the lid can be secured on top for transport or just to keep the bottles cold.

On that note, there are seven openings—to accommodate a six-pack and space in the center for ice. You can also use the cooler for beer cans, two per opening. However, you may want to use a couple long pieces of fabric for each pipe—pop a can down on the fabric and it will be easier to pull out when thirst hits.

HOW YOU MAKE IT

1. Cut the foam insulation board as in the wine rack project, and place the disks in the bottom of the bucket.

2. Cut the PVC pipe into 7 sections, each 10" long.

3. Arrange the pipes in the bucket with one in the center and six spaced equally around the outside (they should sit about ½" below the top edge of the bucket). As with the wine rack, spray about 2" of expanding foam at the base of the pipes, in the spaces between them.

WHAT YOU'LL NEED	**Time** 30 minutes	**Difficulty** Easy	**Expense** $

TOOLS:

Permanent marker, such as a Sharpie

Table saw or hacksaw

Measuring tape

MATERIALS:

Sheet of 2" foam insulation board (4×8")

5-gal. bucket

3" PVC pipe (70" [1.7 m] section)

Expanding foam sealant

VARIATION: **CABLE AND CORD ORGANIZER**

Cables for home computers, peripherals, stereos, and more can lead to annoying visual clutter that ruins the beauty of any room. The chaos of a cable nest also makes sorting out entertainment-center or computer problems a much more difficult task and complicates the process of moving those home electronics to a new room or a new home.

Power cables can be an even worse problem. An extension cord snaking underfoot represents an all-too-real tripping hazard. Unprotected, these cables are at risk of damage that can present other safety issues. Ultimately, controlling cable and cord clutter is just good sense.

A bucket is ideal for organizing these serpentine necessities. The shape allows for the cables or cords to be stored in neat and tidy coils, and a five-gallon bucket can hold a wealth of cables. It can even be used for multiple cables to different electronic components or computer peripherals.

WHAT YOU'LL NEED ⟹ ⟹ ⟹	Time 15 minutes	Difficulty Easy	Expense $

TOOLS:

Cordless drill and bits

80-grit sandpaper

2" (51 mm) hole saw

MATERIALS:

5-gal. bucket with lid

4" PVC slip cap

4" PVC pipe (12" [30.5 cm] section)

(2) ⅜"×¾" Phillips-head crown bolts and nuts

PVC primer

PVC cement

PROJECT OPTIONS

You can stack more than one cord or cable in this manager—just drill access holes at the approximate level of each cable or cord. If you want to separate the cords, you can install the plastic shelf described in the Shelving project, page 21. Do not attach the shelf with screws; just stack it on top of the lower cable. That will allow you easy access to the lower cables, should you need it.

HOW YOU MAKE IT

1. Note the height at which you want the cord to enter the bucket and the height at which the other end will exit it. Transfer these measurements to the outside of the bucket and use a hole saw to drill 2" (51 mm) holes for the ends of the cord to pass through. Sand the inner surface of these holes smooth.

2. Center the PVC cap upside down inside the bucket on the bottom. Use a ⅜" bit to drill two holes inside the cap and through the bottom of the bucket (drill into a scrap piece placed under the bucket).

3. Attach the cap to the bucket with the two crown bolts, hand-tightening the nuts. Prime the inside of the cap rim and the outside of one end of the PVC pipe. Let the primer dry, then coat the inside cap rim and pipe end with PVC cement and slide the pipe into the cap.

4. Once the PVC cement has dried, coil the cable or cord you want to store around the PVC pipe in the bucket. Pull each end of the cable or cord out of the respective holes. Put the lid on the bucket and connect each end of the cable or cord to the outlet or component.

DRYER LINT TRAP

WHAT YOU'LL NEED

TOOLS:

Permanent marker, such as a Sharpie

Cordless drill and bits

Keyhole saw or jigsaw

Tin snips or heavy-duty scissors

Screwdriver

MATERIALS:

5-gal. bucket with lid

Fiberglass replacement screening

Silicone sealant

4" PVC male transition fitting, Schedule 40

5" hose clamp

Time	Difficulty	Expense
25 minutes	Easy	$$

Dryer lint is a small thing that can have big impact. Improperly exhausted dryer lint accounts for tens of thousands of house fires each year, resulting in millions of dollars' worth of damage. And that's just the really scary facts. Even if you fastidiously clean your lint catcher in the dryer, some lint will make it into the venting ductwork. Improperly routed ducting, incorrectly sized vents, and blocked vents can also be the source of problems. Those issues can raise humidity levels around the vent itself, causing moisture to accumulate and mold to grow in the adjacent wall cavity. Lastly, lint that even partially blocks an exhaust hose or vent can drastically decrease the efficiency and lifespan of your dryer.

An efficient external lint trap can be a safety device and insurance against wear and tear on the unit itself. Most dryers are vented to the outside of the home through a screened hole in the wall. This means the dryer has to be located against or near an outer wall. A self-contained lint trap allows you to put the dryer wherever it is most convenient for you, including a basement or utility closet. A water lint trap, such as the one described here, also traps heat from the dryer. You can use this to your advantage in cold weather, to lower your heating bill.

This trap is actually very simple. The dryer vent hose is routed to a five-gallon bucket filled about one-quarter full of water. The water catches and holds most of the lint. A screened section of the lid allows for efficient airflow but prevents any residual lint from flying out of the bucket.

You'll want to make a quick check of local codes—at the zoning and fire departments—to ensure that a self-contained lint trap is permissible in your area. It's also not a wise idea to use an external lint trap so that you can add a washer and dryer to an interior space in a rental, like a closet or alcove. Lastly, under no circumstances should you use this trap with a gas-powered dryer, because it could lead to the buildup of dangerous carbon monoxide.

HOW YOU MAKE IT

1. With the lid fastened on top of the bucket, use the end of the PVC transition fitting as a template to mark a vent hole in the lid of the bucket with the marker. Drill a starter hole and then use the keyhole saw to cut out the hole.

2. Remove the lid and use the saw to cut a half-moon section opposite the hole. This section should be as large as possible. Use the cutout in the lid as a template to mark the half-moon cut on the roll of screening. Use the tin snips or scissors to cut out the half-moon of screening ½" larger all around than the line marked.

3. Lay a generous bead of silicone sealant around the underside of the half-moon cut in the lid, and lay the screen in position. Allow the sealant to fully dry.

4. Lay a bead of silicone around the rim of the vent hole on top of the lid. Set the PVC fitting into place, pushing it through the hole from the top, and laying the flange in the silicone. Allow the silicone to dry.

5. Add 2 gal. of water to the bucket and secure the lid on top. Connect the flexible duct hose from the dryer over the male adapter, using the hose clamp. Dry a load of wet clothes to ensure that air flows freely through the trap and that it is capturing most of the lint.

QUICK 3

THREE QUICK AND USEFUL BUCKET OPTIONS

Whip together a few handy home additions to repurpose any five-gallon buckets lying around. These are all simple solutions to clutter, requiring little time, effort, or expense.

1. Plastic Bag Dispenser

If you're like most people, you have a loose collection of plastic shopping bags. Don't throw them out or let them become a sprawling mess. Cut a hole in the side of a five-gallon bucket, shove them all inside, and you have a handy dispenser.

2. Tool Bucket

Given that it comes with its own handle, a 5-gallon bucket is ideal as a handy-dandy toolbox that will accommodate different sizes and shapes of tools and supplies. It is especially durable in this role. To make the most of the bucket, use the lid. Cut the lid in half and drill holes in one half for the screwdrivers you use the most. Trace slots using the head of your favorite wrenches, and cut out the slots to support those wrenches on the fly. With the modified half-lid in place on the top of the bucket, you can store tools like drills on the inside,

making them convenient to grab, while the top holds your most useful hand tools.

3. Saw Cradle

Even if you have a portable work table, sawing through some work pieces—such as PVC pipe—can be an unwieldy chore. A simple cradle is ideal for making these cuts. Simply mark two deep Vs directly opposite one another on a 5-gallon

bucket's rim. Make the cuts with a jigsaw, and you'll have a portable saw cradle that will hold up to any abuse you can throw at it. You can use it with the lid to transport and hold materials and tools on a job site when not serving as a cradle.

TOY STORAGE CENTER

WHAT YOU'LL NEED

TOOLS:

Cordless drill and bits

MATERIALS:

(2) ½" × 12" (30.5 cm) PVC pipe legs (Schedule 40)

(10) ½" × 10" (25.4 cm) PVC pipe frame supports (Schedule 40)

(4) ½" PVC elbows (Schedule 40)

(4) ½" PVC tees (Schedule 40)

PVC primer and cement

(2) ½" PVC snap (saddle) tees (Schedule 40)

(2) ½" PVC caps (Schedule 40)

(1) ½" PVC cross (Schedule 40)

(4) 5-gal. buckets

Duct tape

#4 ½" (13 mm) flathead wood screws

Time	Difficulty	Expense
60 minutes	Easy	$$

Everyone loves their children, but toy clutter is another matter altogether. It is amazing how many toys children can accumulate, and how many types—and shapes and sizes—there are. Those toys seem to take on a life of their own when it comes to making a mess. Scattered toy cars, blocks, and marbles are probably not the look you had in mind for your home when you picked out the paint and furniture. And it doesn't help that those harmless little playthings can be a danger underfoot. Sadly, getting the kids to pick up after themselves is perhaps the biggest part of the challenge of keeping your living room or play room uncluttered when it's not playtime.

Fortunately, kids can be trained (or coerced, rewarded, or punished) to pick up the mess. Getting them in that habit will be way easier if you have a handy—not to mention fun—toy storage center. The one described in this project provides plenty of room for toys of all kinds—and shapes. Children will find it simple and even a bit fun to literally toss their toys into the storage buckets.

Your room design being of paramount importance, it helps that this particular storage unit is beyond easy to customize. You can paint it and decorate it to blend right in, or go fun and fabulous and make it a centerpiece all its own. Painting or stenciling the framework is as easy as painting the bucket (see **Painting Your Bucket**, page 23). As a bonus, the project will go together with a bare minimum of tools and modifications. The supporting framework has been designed to use off-the-shelf plumbing parts. And the benefits don't stop there. Because the whole structure is crafted of high-density plastic, spills, dirt, and even minor abrasions are a breeze to clean up.

The unit is also scalable. Use the basic principles and parts to expand this storage center to a six-, eight- and even ten-bucket home for toys as needed. If you locate it in a kid's bedroom, designate one bucket for laundry by lining it with a mesh laundry bag and putting a toy basketball hoop over the front of the bucket. You'll kill laundry clutter along with the toy mess!

TOY STORAGE

A toy storage center like this one is only one part of a clutter-free room. To make the most of the storage, you need to motivate children to pick up after themselves. It helps if the storage center is painted in bright, fun colors. Engage your children to pick out the colors, and let them help you paint the frame and buckets.

● Stencil the names of the types of toys to be stored in each bucket. This is a great way for kids of reading age to clearly know where to put what. Emphasize to the children that when things are organized in this way, it's much easier to find their favorite toys.

● For children who don't read, take a picture of each type of toy, print it out, and tape the pictures over the bucket for that type of toy.

● Make a point system. Each time the buckets are full of toys with none left on the floor, the kids get a certain number of points. Anytime toys are left out, points are deducted. When the kids accrue enough points, they get a simple treat.

● Drill air holes in any buckets that hold soft, absorbent toys. This will prevent mold and smells that might keep children from using the bucket for storage.

● Make one bucket just for art supplies. These supplies tend to be messy and hard to find when it comes time to do an art project for school or fun. A single bucket dedicated to arts and crafts confines the mess and makes it easy for children to find what they need.

● Dedicate one bucket to toys for donation. Periodically have your children go through their toys and pull out those they don't play with anymore. These "past their prime" toys go in the donate bucket to be given to charity. That clears space for new birthday and holiday gifts, ensuring there aren't more toys than the storage center can accommodate.

HOW YOU MAKE IT

1. Lay out the PVC frame pieces on the floor, in the position they go together. Working from the bottom, assemble the bottom and first row of vertical supports, connecting the pieces with PVC primer and cement.

2. Connect the top and bottom sections of the frame with a four-way cross in the center of the frame. This is a special-order item that can be found through online PVC specialty outlets and some home centers. If you can't find a cross, create one using standard PVC Schedule 40 slip tees coupled with a snap-on saddle tees.

3. Lay the completed frame on the floor to check alignment and that the frame lies flat. Adjust as necessary.

4. Place the buckets upside down, as they'll be in the frame. Slide the frame, front-side down, over the buckets. Press the frame down and duct tape the bottom cross braces and side braces to each bucket.

5. Flip the unit so that the buckets are right-side up. Drill pilot holes, and drive two ½" screws into the bottom cross brace and two side braces for each bucket.

6. Prime and cement a cap onto one end of each 12" nipple. Slip a snap tee on the opposite end. Position one of these legs on each outside leg. Stand the frame up. To make it stand more upright, move the snap tees down full stop.

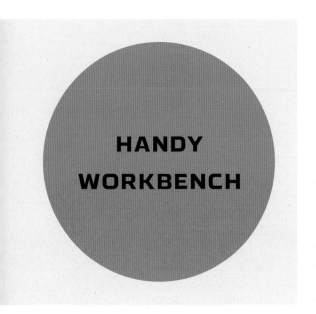

HANDY WORKBENCH

There are few things more useful to the home craftsman (or anyone else, for that matter) than a sturdy, portable work surface. The right workbench is a place to create, craft, fabricate, design, and dream. It should be rugged and durable so that heavy or rough materials won't damage it—the occasional coffee spill or accidental drill-through should not be a big deal. And it should be the right size to fit in a garage or workshop without taking up too much room (but still providing enough space to work comfortably). It should almost be like another tool and quickly become indispensable. That's a lot to ask of one work structure.

The five-gallon bucket delivers. This project, and the specialized variations that follow, provide an easy-setup, easy-breakdown work surface that can be the center of a busy workspace. It serves just as well inside as it does out. Not only will it be the perfect place to do some drilling or sawing, it also makes a wonderful potting table in the yard or garden. It's even great as a staging area for indoor home improvement projects, such as prepping and painting an entire room. (Of course, don't forget, it could serve as the launch pad for many a five-gallon bucket project!)

Portability is a key benefit to this table. You can take it apart in minutes and transport it with ease. That means it can double as a buffet table at a large family cookout or head to the nearest school fundraiser to serve as the base for a display of baked goods. The table can be put together almost entirely from recycled building goods, including empty drywall compound buckets and a beat-up sheet of plywood. Even if you have to buy the components, the low cost is yet another attractive feature of this hardworking surface. The variations on pages 52 and 53 are twists on the main theme outlined in the steps that follow. They allow you to customize this work surface, making it serve your needs no matter what it is you want to do. In any case, though, the surface will be easy to assemble and cheap—much less expensive than buying a workbench or even two high-quality sawhorses.

WHAT YOU'LL NEED

Time	Difficulty	Expense
45 minutes	Easy	$$

TOOLS:

Circular saw or table saw

Measuring tape

Permanent marker, such as a Sharpie

Vise or clamp

Handsaw or jigsaw

MATERIALS:

(8) 5-gal. buckets with lids

Sheet of exterior-grade ½" plywood

HOW YOU MAKE IT

1. Use the circular saw or table saw to rip and cut the plywood down to 20½" wide and 72" long (or use the full 8' length if you prefer a much larger workbench). Measure in 2½" from the edge of one bucket lid and mark with the marker. Use the straightedge to mark a straight line dividing the lid in unequal sections, at the mark.

2. Hold the lid in the vise or clamp it to a work surface so that the cut line is not obstructed. Use a handsaw to cut the lid along the cut line. Repeat the process with three of the remaining lids.

3. To assemble the table, stack one of the buckets with a cut lid on top of a bucket with an uncut lid. Stack two buckets in the same way next to the existing stack. Rotate the top buckets so that the cut portions of the lids align on the outside edges of the buckets. Repeat with the other buckets to create two opposite legs, centered about 4' from the original legs. Set the tabletop in place and move the legs as necessary for better support.

PROJECT OPTIONS

If you want to make the table legs more stable, add weights—such as filled water jugs, bags of sand, or other heavy objects—to the bottom bucket of each leg. To make the table capable of supporting more weight, turn the bottom bucket of each leg upside down and screw the bottoms of both buckets in each leg together.

VARIATION: **SAWHORSE**

Sawhorses are super-handy workshop helpers, adaptable to just about any time you need a work surface right now, right here. This design is better than most because the legs are added storage, helping you lug whatever you need to the job site. Those legs also add a work surface at the end of each crossbeam, making this sawhorse even more useful. Make as many multiples of this design as you might need for a given worksite—they're easy, quick, and inexpensive.

HOW YOU MAKE IT

1. Turn one of the buckets upside down on a work surface. Lay the 2×4 on edge across the center of the bucket bottom, and use it as a template to mark cut lines with the marker. Remove the 2×4 and extend the cut lines 2" down either side of the bucket. Connect the ends of the cuts on each side with a short horizontal cut line.

2. Drill an access hole with the cordless drill, then cut along the cut lines with a jigsaw to remove the section of the bucket bottom in which the end of the 2×4 crossbeam will rest. Repeat with a second bucket.

3. Assemble the sawhorse on a flat surface by stacking the buckets in legs upside down, with the cut buckets on top. The board gaps in the buckets must align. Lay the 2×4 crossbeam in the legs and move the legs as necessary to fully support the 2×4.

WHAT YOU'LL NEED

TOOLS:

Permanent marker, such as a Sharpie

Cordless drill and bits

Hacksaw or jigsaw

Measuring tape

MATERIALS:

2×4 (ideally 6" long, but size as desired)

(4) 5-gal. buckets with lids

Time	Difficulty	Expense
20 minutes	Easy	$

VARIATION: **WORKMATE**

Sometimes, all you need is a small work table to hold a piece of wood or a bucket of paint for a moment. In those situations, there's nothing like this workmate. Set this up in the blink of an eye, and it takes up about as little space as possible, while still providing a stable, modest work surface.

HOW YOU MAKE IT

1. Determine the bottom of the plywood scrap, and measure and mark two perpendicular centerlines. Lay the plywood bottom-side up on a clean, flat work surface.

2. Lay one of the bucket lids top-side down on the plywood, and center it using the centerlines. Drill 3 pilot holes equidistant around the center of the lid, in a triangle. Drill through the lid and into the plywood. Drive the ½" screws through the holes, securing the lid to the plywood.

3. To create your quick-action workmate, snap the lid with attached work surface on one bucket and stack it on the lid of the other bucket.

WHAT YOU'LL NEED 	Time 20 minutes	Difficulty Easy	Expense $

TOOLS:

Measuring tape

Permanent marker, such as a Sharpie

Cordless drill and bits

MATERIALS:

2×2' plywood scrap (at least ¾" thick)

(2) 5-gal. buckets with lids

(3) #4 ½" flathead screws

CHAPTER 2 INTO THE WILD

HEADED OUT CAMPING, HIKING, OR FOR A LONG STAY IN A RUSTIC CABIN IN THE WILDERNESS? DON'T FORGET THE BUCKETS! THE NATURAL DURABILITY AND LIGHT WEIGHT OF A 5-GALLON BUCKET MAKE IT THE PERFECT CHOICE AS AN ACCENT TO YOUR WILDERNESS ADVENTURES. YOU'LL BE AMAZED HOW MANY PURPOSES THIS ADAPTABLE PLASTIC STRUCTURE CAN SERVE IN HELPING MAKE ROUGHING IT SLIGHTLY LESS ROUGH.

Outdoor creations are arguably the best uses for a 5-gallon bucket. It's an ideal size to carry or pack for a wilderness adventure. Where looks don't matter, the sometimes-ugly side of a recycled 5-gallon bucket doesn't play against it. The material also holds up to the worst weather can throw at an outdoorsperson. You'll never need to worry about your bucket collapsing under cold or heat, pouring rain, or even snow.

All the projects in this chapter are eminently usable and incredibly easy to construct. They use some basic principles to provide small luxuries that make any camping or wilderness stay more comfortable, convenient, and enjoyable. Just make sure you bring all your bucket creations home with you because—all the wonderful traits notwithstanding—these buckets do not biodegrade.

CAMPING LIGHT

WHAT YOU'LL NEED

TOOLS:

Cordless drill and bits

1¼" (32 mm) Forstner bit

Permanent marker, such as a Sharpie

Crescent wrench

MATERIALS:

5-gal. bucket with lid (white)

Plastic outdoor floodlight fixture (with cord)

(4) machine screws and nuts

2" rubber fender washer

Silicone adhesive

Replacement LED bulb

Chain or cable and S hook
(optional for hanging)

Time	Difficulty	Expense
20 minutes	Easy	$$

There's a lot to be said about a moonlit campsite in the wild. A small circle of light cast by a tiny campfire can be dreamy and evocative, and looking up at the dots of faraway stars is just one of the many charms of the great outdoors. Unfortunately the charms seem less charming when you trip on the way to get your coat out of the car or have trouble seeing what's making that threatening noise on the edge of camp.

A car-camping or RV campsite is better served with a nicely diffused, soft, general light. Campfires won't cut it. But this wonderful and wonderfully simple camping light will.

The project makes great use of the white plastic's light-diffusing qualities. With a self-contained outdoor light fixture and plenty of extension cord, the light can be hung from just about anywhere you need illumination—a tree, an outbuilding eave, or even your RV. That means you control where the light goes and what areas stay romantically dark.

It doesn't take much to put the light together, and it can double as an additional camping storage container for ropes, the extension cord itself, food, or other necessities. Just make sure whatever bulb you choose is rated for exterior use and well guarded against breakage when you're traveling to and from your outdoor adventure.

HOW YOU MAKE IT

1. Use a 1¼" (32 mm) Forstner bit to drill the plug access hole 2" to 3" (5.1 to 7.6 cm) down from the top edge anywhere on the side of the bucket, below the lowest flange.

2. Remove the lid and place it on a stable, flat sacrificial piece. Center the floodlight's mounting bracket on the underside of the lid and mark the holes for the mounting screws.

3. Drill the mounting screw holes as marked, using the size drill that corresponds to holes. Drill four to six ⅛" (3 mm) vent holes around the edge of the lid and several drain holes in a random pattern in the bucket's bottom.

4. Attach the light fixture base to the underside of the lid with machine screws and nuts. Use a crescent wrench to hold the nuts as the screws are tightened.

5. Push the floodlight fixture plug out through the hole in the side. Slit a rubber washer from the outside edge into the hole. Slip the cord through the slit so that the washer is wrapped around the cord. Pull the cord taut, lay a bead of silicone adhesive around the cord hole in the bucket, and push the washer down over the hole. Let it cure, install the lightbulb, and you're ready to hang your camping light with the chain or cable and S hook.

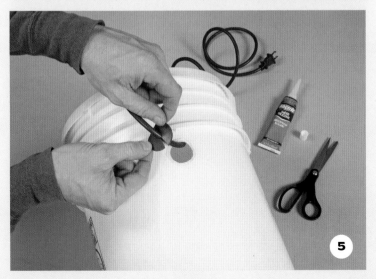

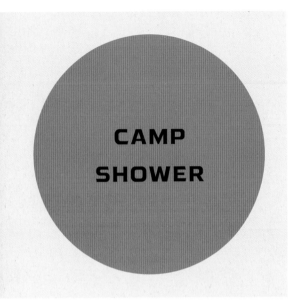

CAMP SHOWER

Anyone who has camped out for even a few days knows that hiking in the woods, hanging around dusty campsites, and just being out in the wild can make any human body pretty ripe. That makes a campground shower not only a luxury but a gift you give to the other campers in your party.

This shower is an improvement on many of the manufactured "solar showers" you can find online and in outdoor shops. First, it has its own carrying handle that not only makes the shower portable but also makes it easy to hang from a sturdy branch (or make use of the solid plastic construction and sit the shower on an embankment or rock outcropping). The nature of the plastic is such that you can either paint the bucket black to heat the water up naturally, or fill it two-thirds full with ambient-temperature water and then boil a big pot of water over the campfire and top off the bucket for a warm and relaxing end-of-day shower. You won't have to worry about the bucket melting or deforming. PVC buckets have no problem with even extremely hot water.

If you fill up the shower to an inch below the rim, you'll be able to enjoy a nine- to ten-minute shower; or several people can have shorter showers. Be aware that you can create a variety of showering experiences based on the showerhead or sprinkler head you buy for the shower. Just keep in mind that changing the head will change how fast the water runs out.

Don't stop at the wilderness's edge. You can use this unit as a pool shower for guests before they jump into your pool. Regardless of what purpose you put it to, it's quick, easy, and inexpensive to build. Not much to ask for a simple outdoor luxury!

TOOLS:

Circular saw

Measuring tape

Cordless drill and bits

7/8" (22 mm) spade bit

Pliers

MATERIALS:

1/2" PVC pipe (Schedule 40)

5-gal. bucket with lid (preferably black or a dark color)

Teflon plumber's tape

1/2" PVC male adapter (Schedule 40)

(2) neoprene or rubber fender washers, 5/8" inside diameter

1/2" PVC female adapter (Schedule 40)

PVC primer and cement

1/2" PVC ball valve (Schedule 40—slip fit)

1/2" PVC male adapter (Schedule 40)

1/2" to 3/4" PVC reducer (Schedule 40)

Spot sprinkler

Chain and S hook

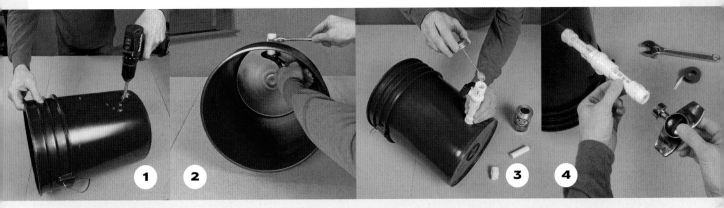

HOW YOU MAKE IT

1. Cut two 1/2" × 3" (7.6 cm) PVC nipples from the 1/2" PVC pipe using a circular saw. Measure 2" (5.1 cm) up from the bottom of the bucket and drill a 7/8" (22 mm) hole with a spade bit.

2. Wrap plumber's tape around the threaded end of the male PVC adapter and stick it through the hole. Slide the O ring over the threaded end, on the inside of the bucket (depending on the adapters you have, you may need more than one to ensure a tight fit). Screw the female adapter onto the male. Tighten the female adapter as tight as possible by hand and then a quarter turn more using pliers.

3. Prime and cement one of the 3" (7.6 cm) PVC nipples into the open end of the male adapter, and into one end of the ball valve. Cement the second nipple into the opposite end of the ball valve.

4. Cement the free end of the nipple into the slip-fit side of the 1/2" to 3/4" reducer. Wrap the threads of the reducer with plumber's tape and screw on the sprinkler head, tightening it hand tight, so that the spray holes face down with the bucket upright.

5. To use the shower, use a chain and an S hook to hang it from a very sturdy branch or other support (or sit it on the edge of a rock ledge). Fill it with water and let the sun heat the water, or leave room and boil a gallon of water, adding it to the bucket right before showering.

BACKPACK

It may not be the most obvious reuse of a 5-gallon bucket, but it is one of the handiest. By using basic tie-down straps, you can convert a durable recycled bucket into an all-purpose carrier that can be hoisted onto your back and taken just about anywhere. This innovation can also serve to make any 5-gallon container much easier to carry when you need to move the contents inside to a faraway or hard-to-reach location.

A bucket strapped securely to your back is a handy way to carry in supplies like food, equipment, or campground staples over uneven territory or through thick forests. That makes this project ideal for the camper, survivalist, or any outdoorsperson who might be going on a short day hike. Once you're in camp, you can even use the emptied bucket to haul freshly caught fish from a river or pond.

Of course, this convenience is just as handy at home. You can pile all manner of tools and supplies in the bucket and carry it to a job site in the far reaches of your backyard or rural property. Just keep in mind that a full 5-gallon bucket can be weighty. Don't try to carry too much unless you have a strong back and sturdy legs.

THE RETAIL OPTION

Even if you're not feeling up to fabricating your own 5-gallon bucket backpack, you can make use of the storage potential with a manufactured nylon frame that wraps around the bucket. These products are well padded and easy to secure in place around the bucket. At least two manufacturers produce these products and possibly more. You can find them online at a cost of $25 to $35.

TOOLS:

Measuring tape

Permanent marker, such as a Sharpie

Level

Bar clamps

Cordless drill and bits

Jigsaw

Rat-tail file or 80-grit sandpaper

MATERIALS:

5-gal. bucket with lid

(2) nylon ratcheting tie-down straps (38" [96.5 cm] or longer)

Rubber gasket kit (optional)

Flathead machine screws and nuts

HOW YOU MAKE IT

1. Clean the bucket thoroughly. Measure and mark for the top strap slots. The top slots are located 1" (2.5 cm) below the lowest flange around the mouth of the bucket and 8" (20.3 cm) apart at the inside edges. The slots are ¼" (6 mm) high and 2½" (6.4 cm) wide.

2. Use a level to mark the bottom slots on a plumb vertical line with the top slots. The bottom slots are located 2" (5.1 cm) up from the bottom. They are also ½" (1.3 cm) top to bottom and 2½" (6.4 cm) wide but are slanted slightly so that the inside edges are lower than the outside edges.

3. Stabilize the bucket with clamps, and drill ½" (13 mm) holes at either end of each marked slot. Use a jigsaw to finish cutting out the slots. Use a fine rat-tail file or sandpaper to clean up each slot. Smooth all the edges so that they don't wear on the straps.

4. Guide a tie-down strap through each set of upper and lower strap slots. Try the backpack on and adjust the straps to fit the most comfortable position.

Optional: If the bucket presses into your back, attach the pads from a rubber gasket kit or cut pieces of an old yoga mat at the top and bottom of the bucket, centered between the straps. Drill ⅜" (10 mm) holes through the pads and bucket, and bolt the pads in place with flathead machine screws and nuts.

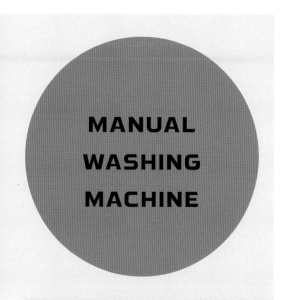

MANUAL WASHING MACHINE

WHAT YOU'LL NEED

TOOLS:

Cordless drill and bits, including 1½" (38 mm) spade bit

MATERIALS:

5-gal. bucket with lid

Cup plunger with 6" or larger head

80-grit sandpaper

Plastic water dispenser replacement spigot

Silicone sealant (optional)

Time	Difficulty	Expense
15 minutes	Easy	$

Eventually, we all need clean clothes. But few people enjoy laundry day. That's why washing machines are such a wonderful modern convenience. Just throw a load (or, in many cases, less than a load) into the unit, turn it on, and presto—clean clothes. The downside is that these magnificent machines are energy and water hogs. Depending on how new and what type your washing machine is, it can use between 15 and 45 gallons of water per load!

Ironically these machines use amazingly sophisticated technology to perform a rudimentary process that hasn't changed much in centuries. The basic principle of that process involves agitating dirty clothes in soapy water for a prescribed period of time. Use warm water for colorfast clothing and white textiles, and cold or warm water for garments with colors that might bleed. Rinse in the same temperature. Basically that's all there is to it.

Truth is, that process is so simple that it can easily be done with a manual washing machine. The one described here will be highly effective at getting clothes clean without a power source. It's an ideal convenience in the event that your home loses power for a significant period of time, or if you go on a lengthy RV camping trip. Whether you're staying in a cabin, a camper, or a tent, or just want to simplify your homestead, having a manual washing machine at your disposal means you don't have to have quite as many clothes.

The other benefit is exercise. So many people pay for a gym when you can get a decent workout just by saving electricity and water. Even the least fit person in the household will be quite capable of washing a small load of clothes, while burning a tidy sum of calories. You can even operate the washer described here while sitting down if need be, or it can be used on a table or other raised surface so that someone with back problems doesn't have to bend over.

Whatever the case, because the whole idea is environmental friendliness, it's best if you use biodegradable soap to maintain the green cred of this appliance. That way, you can reuse the water in a nonedible part of your garden.

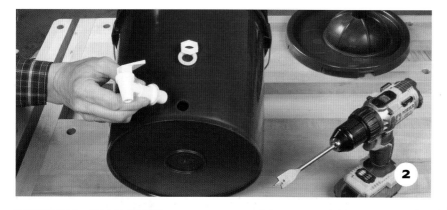

HOW YOU MAKE IT

1. With the lid secured on the bucket, use the spade bit to drill a hole in the center of the lid. Check to see that the plunger handle will slide through the hole with a fair amount of play, allowing it to be moved around inside the bucket. Sand the edges of the hole smooth so that they don't abrade the plunger handle.

2. Drill a $7/16$" hole (or use the appropriate bit size for the spigot you're using) in the side of the bucket, as close to the bottom as possible. Fasten the water dispenser replacement spigot in the hole, tightening it enough to ensure a good seal.

3. Drill 6 to 8 holes $3/8$" in diameter in a random pattern on the rubber cup of the plunger. Test the washer by adding a small load of clothes, filling with water and a small amount of detergent, and plunging the load. Move the plunger around to ensure complete agitation. After 10 to 15 minutes, drain the water through the spigot and refill with clean water. Agitate again and drain. Repeat as necessary. If the spigot leaks, empty the bucket, let it dry, and lay a bead of silicone sealant around the outside rim of the spigot. Let the sealant dry, then fill the bucket with water and check that it no longer leaks before using.

MANUAL WASHING MACHINE TIPS

This is a very simple device, but one that needs to be used correctly if you're going to get your clothes clean with a minimum of effort. The following guidelines will help you do that:

● Use only biodegradable laundry detergent. The whole point of this simple machine is to save electricity and water, and it should be used as a green water source.

● You need only a little detergent; many people use too much laundry detergent. Keep in mind that the capacity of this washing machine is much less than a standard house-hold unit. A tablespoon of detergent should be plenty. Coupled with vigorous agitation, your clothes will be as clean as ever.

● Disassemble the machine and let the parts dry between laundry days. If you leave the lid on while the machine is wet, mold can grow in the bucket.

ROCKET STOVE

A rocket stove is just about the simplest cooking device you can construct. It is extremely basic—nothing more than a tube with an L bend that serves as a firebox for small-diameter fuel such as twigs or wood chips. The stove's temperature can't be modulated; it runs hot and cooks food quickly.

A rocket stove is ideal for car camping, an ice-fishing adventure, or even a modest cookout in the backyard if you don't have an outdoor grill (or on the fire escape, if you don't have a backyard). It takes very little time and effort to construct and is remarkably inexpensive.

Be aware that some crafters and homesteaders make this stove out of 5-gallon PVC buckets. That's certainly easy to do, but this project opts for extra-safety in the form of a metal 5-gallon bucket. You can use your own judgment in which material you choose.

In either case, cooking with a rocket stove is a breeze. Load up the tube, light the starter fuel (usually newspaper or dried leaves), and throw your food right over the chimney outlet. Keep a close eye on whatever you cook because it won't take long to be ready. And keep in mind that this is essentially an open flame—use all the fire safety you would exercise if you were thinking about having an open campfire. Keep in mind that some campsites and wild areas don't permit the use of rocket stoves.

1

3

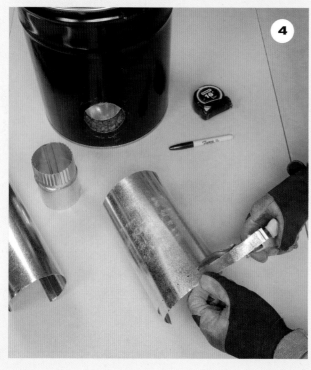

4

6

WHAT YOU'LL NEED

Time	Difficulty	Expense
30 minutes	Moderate	$$

TOOLS:

Measuring tape

Permanent marker, such as a Sharpie

Cordless drill and bits

Jigsaw with steel-cutting blade

Tin snips

Metal file

Trowel

MATERIALS:

5-gal. steel bucket

3" galvanized steel 90° round elbow

Pea gravel

3" galvanized steel chimney stove flue pipe

Sheet metal screws

Replacement charcoal grate

HOW YOU MAKE IT

1. Use one end of the galvanized steel elbow as a template to trace a circle 2" (5.1 cm) above the bottom of the bucket. Cut the circle out by drilling an access hole and using a jigsaw equipped with a steel-cutting blade to make the cut.

2. Add pea gravel to the bottom of the bucket, up to the bottom of the hole. Sit the elbow directly in the center of the bottom with one inlet pointed toward the hole, and the other pointed upward.

3. Measure from the inlet inset up to the lip and note the distance. Do the same from the bottom inlet inset to the hole in the side of the bucket, and add 3" (7.6 cm).

4. Use the measurements to cut two sections of 3" galvanized steel chimney stove flue pipe. Use tin snips for this. Snap the sections into tubes if they aren't already. *Note: When working with sheet metal pipe and a metal 5-gallon bucket, it's important to wear cut-proof gloves and file all cut surfaces smooth to prevent injury.*

5. Position the elbow in the bottom of the bucket with the bottom inlet pointed toward the hole in the side of the bucket. Insert the lower, shorter tube, through the hole and into the elbow inlet. Slide the upper draft tube into the elbow inlet that is pointed up. Use sheet metal screws at each connection to secure the sections.

6. Hold the tube in place as you use a trowel to fill around the tube with pea gravel. Level the pea gravel around the mouth of the tube.

7. Set a metal grate on top of the rocket stove. Test out the stove by lining the bottom of the lower fuel tube with crumbled newspaper or similar starter. Jam in twigs, lumber offcuts (but not pressure treated), and other small fuel, and light the newspaper on fire. The heat should immediately draft up out of the top of the stove, ready for cooking.

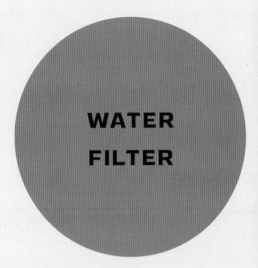

WATER FILTER

3

A homemade water filter is an awfully handy addition to your home backup supplies. The filter can be essential in an emergency, such as a flood or earthquake, where the existing water supply may be compromised. But a high-volume water filter is also a lifesaver in the event that a well that serves as a primary source of drinking water for the house becomes contaminated or otherwise unusable. If you're willing to portage it in, this appliance can also serve you well for filtering stream, river, or even lake water that you suspect is not drinkable.

The water filter described here uses three gravity-feed-activated charcoal-and-ceramic filters. You'll find a wide range of these on the market, but the "candle" style (see Resources, page 144) used in this project is the most common for homemade filtration systems. The difference between different filters on the market is what they filter out. More expensive models will remove even trace amounts of industrial chemicals and heavy metals. Most of them will remove larger particulates and more common contaminants such as lead.

If you are concerned that the water you're filtering may contain microbes or particulates that your filters don't treat, you can use one of two methods for secondary purification. Either boil the filtered water for 5 minutes at an active rolling boil, or add eight drops of chlorine bleach per gallon of water, and let the water sit, uncovered, for at least 1 hour before drinking it. You can also combine these two for even more protection. Either way, thoroughly test the water filter long before you have a need to use it.

TOOLS:

Cordless drill and bits

Groove joint pliers (optional)

MATERIALS:

Permanent marker, such as a Sharpie

(2) food-grade, clean 5-gal. buckets with lids and handles

(3) gravity-feed, candle-style water filters

Plastic water dispenser replacement spigot

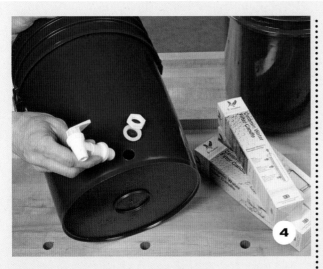

HOW YOU MAKE IT

1. On the underside of one of the bucket lids, mark three holes in a triangle around the center of the lid. The holes should be separated from each other by about 5".

2. Turn one of the buckets upside down and center the marked lid, upside down, over the bottom of the bucket. Use a 7/16" bit to drill holes at the three marks, through the lid and the bucket bottom. (Or use the drill bit size that corresponds to the nubs on the filters you are using.)

3. Working from inside the bucket, push the mounting post of one filter through a hole in the bottom, and through the corresponding hole in the lid. Tighten the filter in place using the supplied wing nut. Hand tighten the nut until it is very snug. Repeat with the remaining filters. Fill the bucket with about ½ gal. of water and let stand to check for leaks. If you detect any leaks, tighten the mounting nuts until the seal is secure.

4. Mark a hole in the second bucket on the side, 1" up from the bottom, for the spigot. Use the post of the spigot as a template to mark the hole, and then use the appropriate bit to drill the hole. Snug the nut on the spigot to ensure a tight seal (using pliers if necessary), and then fill the bucket with water to just above the spigot and check for leaks.

5. Prime the filters as necessary, according to the manufacturer's instructions. Place the bucket and lid holding the filters on the lower bucket, and snap the lid in place. Fill the top bucket with 5 gal. of water and run this load through the filters and discard. You're now ready to filter contaminated water. The 3 filters should process 1 gal. of water every 15 minutes.

RABBIT TRAP

Want to survive in the wild? You're going to need protein and plenty of it. Unfortunately the forest doesn't offer stacks of protein powder, but it does contain some slow-moving critters that make for a good meal. This simple trap will capture you some of the most delicious. But even if you're not a hunter—and maybe not even a meat eater—you can still use this to trap and move furry thieves that are ravaging a garden patch and taking more than their due.

The theory is pretty simple. The trap is baited with some greens and a couple juicy carrots, and the prey hops into the bucket hoping for a free meal. The pivot on the bottom means that as the rabbit moves to the back of the bucket to enjoy dinner, the mouth of the bucket tilts up, the post holding the lid open drops, and bingo! Bugs is trapped.

There are a number of ways you can modify this for the situation. No pivot? No worries. Dig a small hole and balance the bucket trap on the edge. It will fall backwards into the hole with the bunny

inside and unable to get out. The number of ways you can use this trap are limited only by your imagination.

However, do your best to disguise the bucket and blend it in with the surroundings. Using a green bucket is a good idea, as is spreading some young branches over the bucket. Beyond that, all you need is patience. Most rabbit hunters set the trap and check back later.

TOOLS:

Measuring tape

Permanent marker, such as a Sharpie

Miter saw

Cordless drill and bits

MATERIALS:

5-gal. bucket with lid

(3) ½" × 15" (38.1 cm) PVC pipe for stakes (Schedule 40)

½" × 12" (30.5 cm) PVC pipe for post (Schedule 40)

1¼"× 15" (38.1 cm) PVC pipe for pivot (Schedule 40)

(2) 1" (25 mm) screws

(3) 4" (10.2 cm) zip ties

Heavy-duty rubber band

(2) 8" (20.3 cm) zip ties

HOW YOU MAKE IT

1. Measure, mark, and cut with a miter saw three 15" (38.1 cm) stakes from ½" PVC pipe. Miter one end of each stake 22.5 degrees. Cut a 12" (30.5 cm) post from the pipe. Cut a 15" (38.1 cm) piece of 1¼" PVC pipe.

2. With the lid on the bucket, drill three ¼" (6 mm) holes 2" (5.1 cm) apart along the lip (through both the lid and the bucket). Drill a ¼" (6 mm) hole in the lid, exactly opposite the centermost of the three previous holes. On the opposite side of the bucket (what will be the bottom when the trap is set), 2" (5.1 cm) up from bottom, drive two 1" (25 mm) screws 2" (5.1 cm) apart into the inside of the bucket. The points of these will be used to hold the carrots to bait the trap, preventing them from rolling forward.

3. Remove the lid and wire it to the bucket by running three 4" (10.2 cm) zip ties through the holes and tightening the ties to create a hinge.

Secure one end of a heavy-duty rubber band through the matching hole in the bucket rim, looping it in itself. Secure the other end through the single hole opposite the other three in the lid, holding it in place with a dowel, small twig, or similar method.

4. To set up the trap, lay the bucket on its side with the lid's zip-tie hinge at the top. Drive a stake on either side, roughly at the center of the bucket and one behind the bucket. Slide the PVC pipe that will serve as a pivot under the bucket and in back of the two stakes on the sides. Use the 8" (20.3 cm) zip ties to tie the pivot to the stakes. Stick carrots in the holes in the bottom of the bucket, and scatter greens around the carrots. Lean the bucket forward on the pivot and prop the lid open with the post so that the post is at an angle. Scatter greens around the mouth of the bucket, and wait for your quarry!

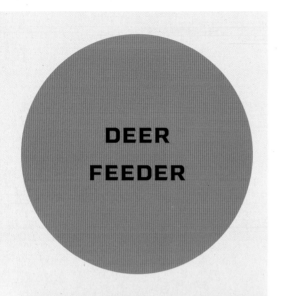

DEER FEEDER

WHAT YOU'LL NEED

TOOLS:

Measuring tape

Permanent marker, such as a Sharpie

Handsaw

Cordless drill and bits

Jigsaw

MATERIALS:

(2) 3" × 17" (43.2 cm) PVC pipe sections
(Schedule 40)

5-gal. bucket with lid

80-grit sandpaper or fine file

(4) ½" self-tapping screws

Time	Difficulty	Expense
30 minutes	Moderate	$

The idea with this project is to provide food for deer in the fall and winter when natural food sources may be limited. Naturalists use deer feeders to draw deer for wildlife watching. Hunters use them to not only draw more deer into the hunting area but also increase the size and score (number of antler points on the bucks) of the deer that are there. Whatever the goal, feeders can help deer populations make it through harsh winters (but there are feeder opponents, and reasons for not using them in some areas—see box opposite. In some cases, it's wise to add a protein powder supplement to the corn feed to make sure deer diets aren't too heavy on carbohydrates.

The feeder in this project is a simple version—easy to construct, easy to place, and easy to use. The design is far less complicated than bump feeders that are constructed with a valve and a bump weight that releases small amounts of corn on the ground as deer nudge it. Those make for a more natural feeding experience for a larger group of deer, but deer will certainly enjoy the bounty this one offers. In any case, the feed used is the same: large-kernel dried corn.

Like any other wildlife feeder, it's essential to keep this one clean and stocked. That is partially a consequence of where you put it and how you maintain it. In any case, placement is crucial. It should be near water and wherever the deer bed down, far from human foot and vehicle traffic; and, of course, it also has to be relatively accessible so that you can regularly refill the feeder.

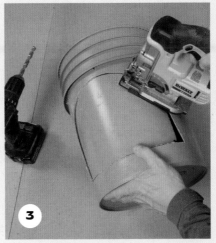

HOW YOU MAKE IT

1. Measure, mark, and cut with a handsaw two sections of 3" PVC pipe 17" (43.2 cm) long (or about ½" (1.3 cm) shorter than the height of the bucket you are using). Measure and mark one end of each section for a 45" miter (measure up from one end approximately 2½" [6.4 cm] and mark the cut to down to the end; the miter does not need to be precise). Cut the miter with a sharp handsaw, working slowly and carefully.

2. Measure and mark the feeder window cutout, orienting it parallel with the handle. Start by marking an 11" (28 cm) line around the body of the bucket, 2½" (6.4 cm) up from the bottom. Measure 8" to 10" (20.3 to 25.4 cm) up from the center of this line. Mark two arcing lines from the top point down to either end of the bottom line. You can do this freehand or create a template out of thick sketch paper or cardboard and tape it in place as a guide.

3. Drill an access hole and cut out the feed window with a jigsaw. Use a blade meant for cutting plastic, with at least ten teeth per inch. Use 80-grit sandpaper or a fine file to clean up the cut edges around the window.

4. Stick one of the feed pipes down into the bucket, with the miter on the bottom. Make sure the mouth of the miter is facing the inside of the bucket, and then drive ½" self-tapping screws from the outside of the bucket into the pipe to hold it in place. Drive one close to the top and one near the bottom. Repeat the process with the second pipe so that it's opposite the first pipe.

5. Clean out the feeder to remove any remaining small plastic pieces. Fill the feed pipes with corn (it should flow into the feed tray and then backup into the pipes). Secure the lid on top and hang the feeder near deer trails or clearings where deer gather.

FEEDER DEBATE

Although used widely by hunters, several states outlaw the use of deer feeders for their negative impacts on some deer populations. One of the key problems is that a large number of deer can be drawn into a relatively small area if they come to rely on a feeder. That concentration can spread disease, such as the deadly chronic wasting disease that has decimated deer populations in several states. Deer feed is also purely carbohydrates, and, depending on what other food is available in the local area, the corn alone may be an unhealthy diet. So much so, that a condition called *acidosis* can kill deer that eat exclusively carbohydrates for months. The wisest course of action is to call your state Department of Fish and Wildlife. The officials there can offer guidance on any state laws that prohibit feeders and what wildlife professionals consider the best practices for the local region.

CHAPTER 3

CRITTER CARE

THE ANIMALS IN OUR LIVES DESERVE OUR ATTENTION AND CARE. NOT ONLY IS IT THE HUMANE THING TO DO; IT MAKES LIFE SIMPLER. BY ENSURING THE HEALTH, WELL-BEING, AND HAPPINESS OF ANIMALS UNDER YOUR ROOF OR LODGED OUT IN YOUR YARD, YOU CAN AVOID VET BILLS.

When it comes to the animals we keep for food, care and tending are even more important. Keep your chickens happy, for instance, and you ensure a steady supply of eggs. Those eggs will usually be healthier than what you can pick up from the local grocery store. Over time you may even realize a cost savings on your grocery bill—or you can impact your bottom line by raising chicks for sale.

No matter what, animal husbandry involves making your feathered and furry charges comfortable. Mostly that's about feeding, but it's also about physical comfort, from providing a safe and cozy place for hens to nest, to making sure cats have a private indoor space they can call their very own bathroom.

The great part about all the innovations in this chapter is that they help you toward those goals while being quick, easy, and inexpensive to achieve. All these creations fit right in with the idea of homesteading and sustainable living, especially if you make them with reused buckets. On that note, remember that many of these projects have to do with feeding animals. Use food-grade buckets, or those that can be thoroughly cleaned, for those projects. Do not use buckets that were used to hold chemicals, such as those for pool chemicals or industrial operations.

CHICKEN FEEDER

WHAT YOU'LL NEED

TOOLS:

Permanent marker, such as a Sharpie

Measuring tape

Cordless drill and bits

1½" (38 mm) hole saw

Crescent wrench

Standard screwdriver

MATERIALS:

Clean 5-gal. bucket with a threaded hole in the lid and a screw-on top

(3) ¼" stove bolts and nuts with washers

Metal, plastic, or rubber garbage can lid (no handle)

Time	Difficulty	Expense
30 minutes	Easy	$

Feeding chickens everyday isn't the worst chore ever, but it doesn't really need to be a chore at all. You can save some time and effort by constructing a fill-it-and-forget-it chicken feeder. You'll need to fill this handy clucker accessory only about once every seven to ten days for a small flock of ten chickens. The trick to the feeder is to let gravity do the work. And because the bucket used in this feeder is positioned right-side up, you can use the handle to hang the unit up off the ground (the preferred strategy for a number of reasons—see **Safety First** on page 80). You'll need a clean bucket that has an opening in the lid equipped with a screw-on top, like the pour spout in a five-gallon bucket of paint. That way, you won't have to wrestle the bucket's lid off when it comes time to refill the feeder—just unscrew the top and add chicken feed through a funnel. Make this at home following the steps below and you'll be saving a whole lot of money—store-bought versions of chicken feeders can run from $35 to $60!

You can save even more money by reusing found materials. Although we've used a plastic garbage can lid for both the feeder and the alternative projects that follow, a rubberized oil pan or even a roasting pan would work just as well. However, it's wise to stay away from materials that are prone to rust or corrosion. And keep in mind that chickens tend to climb on and jostle structures in their environment; the more rigid and durable any material you use for a feeder or watering basin, the better.

Lastly, whether you choose to hang the feeder or just sit it on the ground, we suggest you put it outside the coop to help keep the coop nice and clean. (Chickens are messy eaters!) The waterer, on the other hand, can go inside the coop so that the birds always have access to a fresh, clean water source.

HOW YOU MAKE IT

1. Mark 4 holes 1" up from the bottom of the bucket, equidistant around the bucket's perimeter. Secure the bucket upside down, with a weight on the bottom (or clamp it in a large vise), and drill the holes using the 1½" hole saw.

2. Mark 3 holes on the top of the garbage can lid, in a triangle with each hole approximately 3" from the center. Drill ¼" holes at the marks. Center the lid over the upside-down bucket and mark corresponding holes on the bucket's bottom. Remove the lid and drill ¼" holes at the marks on the bottom of the bucket.

3. Attach the lid to the bottom of the bucket using 3 stove bolts, with the bolt heads on the lid side. Place a washer under both the head and the nut on each bolt. Tighten the nuts securely.

4. Turn the bucket right-side up, so that it's sitting in the upturned lid. Install a screw-top lid with separate frame, as shown here, or simply use a snap-on lid with a pour hole and cap. Unscrew the pour-hole screw top and fill the bucket with chicken feed. Let the chickens know it's dinnertime!

VARIATION: **CHICKEN WATERER**

Chicken owners are increasingly turning away from traditional watering troughs to newer, more sanitary "nipple feeders." These feature simple nipple valves that the chicken pecks for a quick drink. Because the water is kept in a closed container and the nipple ensures a seal, many advocates consider this a good way to ensure the water source never becomes contaminated. Most chickens figure out the nipple system almost immediately. You'll be using push-in nipple feeders (these can be found at any large feed or supply store, or online—do not buy screw-in styles); follow the instructions supplied with your nipples. Use a chain and an S hook to keep the waterer off the ground so that chickens don't step in it and foul the water.

CHICKEN-FEEDING TIPS

Whether they're getting their feed from a feeder or directly off the ground, chickens naturally scratch when they feed. This means that chickens may stand in a feeder on the ground, flicking food out while eating. If this becomes a problem, use a deeper feeder base, replacing the garbage can lid in this project with a plastic oil pan or similar container. Of course, you can also hang the feeder by its handle. Here are a few more tips to keep your birds well fed:

● If you're supplementing your chickens' feed with a calcium source, such as crushed oyster shells, put it in a separate feeder or dish. (Ironically crushed eggshells are a wonderful calcium supplement for chicken feed!)

● When molting, chickens may need additional protein sources. Add mealworms to their food.

● Add 1 tablespoon of raw, unfiltered apple-cider vinegar to the chickens' water to eliminate potentially harmful bacteria.

WHAT YOU'LL NEED

TOOLS:

Cordless drill and bits

MATERIALS:

5-gal. bucket with lid

(3) or (4) push-in style watering nipples with grommets

Time	Difficulty	Expense
15 minutes	Easy	$

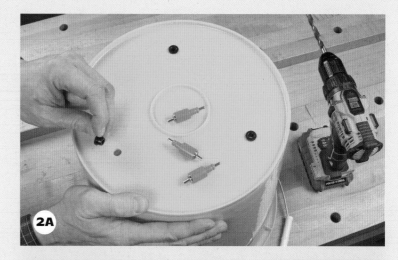

2A

2B

SAFETY FIRST

To keep chickens healthy, make sure that they are not defecating in a feeder or waterer. Hanging is a sure solution to the problem, but regularly empty and thoroughly clean the bucket feeder and waterer to ensure against harmful contaminants such as mold. Keep waterers off the ground where there are chicks roaming freely. They can fall in and drown.

HOW YOU MAKE IT

1. Turn the bucket upside down and drill 3 to 4 holes distributed in a triangular or square pattern across the bottom of the bucket.

2. Wet one of the supplied grommets and push it into the hole (A). Then push a nipple in through the grommet until you feel it seat. Repeat with the remaining nipples (B) and then fill the bucket with water and check that the nipples are working correctly (a drop of water should come out when you depress the nipple).

VARIATION: CHICKEN WATERER 2

If for any reason you can't find watering nipples or prefer not to use them, you can still keep your feathered egg machines hydrated. This innovation works on simple hydrodynamic principles, which require that the lid fit tightly, creating an airtight seal. (An airtight seal at the top is what prevents water from just flowing out of the holes and up over the rim of the base.) It's essential to use a bucket with a hole in the lid equipped with a screw-on top, so that you can easily refill the waterer. As with the feeder, the bucket handle allows this device to be hung.

HOW YOU MAKE IT

1. Secure the bucket upside down. Cut or drill a ½" hole in the side, right at the bottom edge. Center the garbage can lid over the bottom. Drill a ¼" hole through the center of the garbage can lid and into the bucket.

2. Secure the lid to the bucket with a stove bolt and nut. Use a rubber washer on both sides, under the bolt head and under the nut. Lay a small bead of silicone sealant underneath each rubber washer before tightening the nut, and bolt down as tight as possible without cracking the bucket.

3. Allow the silicone to dry. Hang the waterer in the most convenient area for the chickens (inside the coop if there is space). Use a hose to fill the bucket about ¾ full, through the hole in the lid. Quickly screw down the top on the fill hole. Check for leaks and fill with sealant as necessary.

WHAT YOU'LL NEED	Time 30 minutes	Difficulty Easy	Expense $

TOOLS:
Cordless drill and bits

½" (13 mm) bit

Crescent wrench

Standard screwdriver

MATERIALS:
Clean 5-gal. bucket with an opening and screw-on top in the lid

¼" stove bolt and nut

Plastic or rubber garbage can lid (no handle)

(2) rubber washers

Silicone sealant

EGG INCUBATOR

This project is a very basic incubator design. The point is to provide a good environment for the chicks-in-development while keeping costs low. The thrift translates to a minimum of effort that would otherwise be automated. That extra work gives you a chance to interact with the birds you're hatching and regularly check the health of the eggs. The capacity is modest, meant to hatch no more than five eggs at a time. That said, you can modify the design to match your preferences and expertise. It's easy to add an automatic egg turner, a thermostat with a switch to turn the lamp on and off based on temperature, and fans to circulate air and heat more evenly and efficiently.

The most important factor is a steady temperature. Chicken eggs incubate at about 99 to 102 degrees Fahrenheit. (If you want to incubate eggs of other species of birds or reptiles, investigate the ideal temperature for that particular species.) Humidity is important as well. The ideal humidity for the inside of a chicken egg incubator is about 60 percent. That means you'll need a water source inside the unit.

For this project, you'll want a location with an electrical outlet, out of the way of foot traffic, and where curious pets and other animals can't get at the eggs (or break the incubator trying). A dark corner of a shed or the garage is ideal, especially where the temperature doesn't fluctuate radically over the course of the day. Keep the unit out of direct sunlight, which can quickly overheat the incubator. There are many acceptable surfaces on which to sit the incubating eggs; this unit uses the inexpensive straw you'd find in a chicken's nest. The eggs should be placed in the straw with their pointed ends down, and you must regularly move them. Turn the eggs once or a twice a day, if possible, to ensure healthy chicks. The eggs should be placed on their sides right before they hatch.

Finally, don't be impatient. The typical incubation period for chicken eggs is 21 days, but that's just a guideline—some eggs will take longer. Don't be shocked if the occasional egg doesn't hatch; industrial poultry operations hatch only about 80 to 90 percent of their eggs.

TOOLS:

Permanent marker, such as a Sharpie

Frameless hacksaw

Utility knife

Cordless drill and bits

MATERIALS:

Lamp socket with separate threaded rim or flange, cord, and in-line switch

Analog probe-style air conditioning thermometer (or equivalent)

Clean 5-gal. bucket with lid

Silicone sealant

Foam insulation board

Automotive cup holder

(2) #4 ½" flathead screws

75-watt light

INCUBATING EGG AFTER-CARE

Incubating eggs is a fantastic way to turn fertilized eggs into new chickens. You don't need a whole lot of specialized knowledge or the services of a veterinarian, but successfully incubating chicken eggs does take a fair amount of care and attention to details. The more TLC you lavish on incubating eggs, the more eggs that hatch in reward for your efforts. Ideally check eggs during the process several times per day. Pay particular attention to the following:

● **WATER LEVEL.** The cup in the cup holder should be at least half full of water at all times. This is essential because humidity plays a key role in chick development during incubation. Chances are, you'll encounter a lot of conflicting advice about humidity. Some experts recommend starting out with around 40 percent humidity for the first sixteen to eighteen days, increasing to around 60 percent for the remainder of incubation, but this incubator shoots for a constant level of humidity. Use an inexpensive hygrometer to monitor humidity in the incubator. The optimal humidity for your eggs depends on several factors—from local climate to the variations in heat in your incubator. If your hatch rate is low, you may want to add a second cup holder (although high humidity can be as bad as low).

● **TEMPERATURE.** Internal temperature should not vary by more than 1 or 2 degrees. Check the thermometer often; if the temperature starts to climb too high, turn off the lightbulb. If it falls too low, use duct tape to cover the air vents until the temperature returns to normal.

● **TURNING THE EGGS.** Egg movement ensures healthy chicks. Turning the eggs several times each day is recommended. If this becomes impossible, you can purchase an aftermarket egg turner.

● **SANITATION.** Clean the incubator thoroughly between batches of eggs, with soapy water and a rinse of bleach in warm water. Also replace the straw for each new batch of eggs.

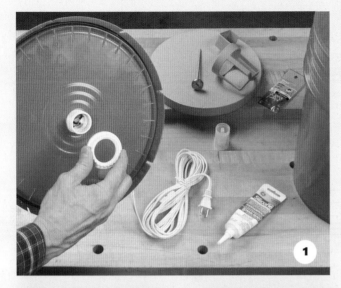

HOW YOU MAKE IT

1. Hold the lamp socket upside down, centered on the top of the bucket lid. Use the marker to trace around the post of the lamp socket, then cut out the hole with the frameless hacksaw. Push the socket through the hole so that it is sitting on its rim, and screw the flange on top. Lay a bead of silicone sealant around the edge of the flange before pressing it down into position.

2. Use the bottom of the bucket to trace a circle on the insulation board. Cut inside the traced line with a utility knife. Place the foam insulation circle in the bottom of the bucket.

3. Use the utility knife or hacksaw to cut the hanging lip off the cup holder. Position the cup holder along the inside wall of the bucket, with the top about 4" below the top of the bucket. Drill 2 pilot holes through the tang of the cup holder out through the bucket. Fasten the cup holder in place by driving 2 flathead screws in from the outside through the pilot holes.

4. Opposite the cup holder and 6" from the bottom of the bucket, drill an access hole for the thermometer probe. The drill bit should be the same size as the probe or just slightly smaller. Apply a generous bead of silicone sealant around the outside of the hole, and then push the thermometer through the hole and seat the back of the dial in the sealant.

5. Drill 3 vent holes ⅜" in diameter equidistant around the outside of the bucket, about 5" from the top. To set up the incubator, spread about 2" of loose straw in the bottom of the bucket. Put a paper cup full of water in the cup holder. Plug in the light and snap the lid on the bucket. When the thermometer shows that the temperature is about 99°F, remove the top and place the eggs in the straw, pointed side down.

VARIATION: **NESTING BOX**

When you're looking to get the most out of your chickens, there are a lot of advantages to a nesting box. A properly constructed and sited nesting box keeps hens comfortable and laying in one clean and handy place, instead of in the grass outside or other places where eggs can become contaminated or break. This makes gathering eggs much easier and ensures your yield will be as high as possible. Properly trained, the hens will always use the nesting box (see Nesting Box Rules, page 86). The box serves the chicken owner, as well—no more hunting for eggs!

Although it seems like a simple structure, a nesting box has certain requirements if it is going to be used as it should be. This particular box is ideal, even though once you put it in place it may seem a little confining. Too much space means hens spend too much time in the box, and that usually translates to a lower number of eggs laid.

The advantages to using a five-gallon bucket go far beyond size, though. The structure is already enclosed, giving hens a sense of privacy and safety. Like any vulnerable creature, hens like to feel secure,

especially when they are laying. The shape of the bucket also suits nesting perfectly. The bucket is, by its nature, adaptable and cleanable—an essential trait whenever you're building something for use by chickens.

You'll quickly know that your nesting box is successful by certain very apparent signs. First and foremost, the chickens should lay their normal number of eggs—or more if they really respond well to the box. Also, if the nesting box is reinforcing behavior as it should (and you're doing the same with how you treat the chickens), hens won't defecate in the box. They also won't peck at the eggs—a sure sign that they are not comfortable in a nesting box. More importantly, they won't lay outside of the nesting box.

If your chickens are a little reluctant to use the new nesting box, you can get them started with a little fake-out. Place a ceramic egg or even a golf ball inside the nesting box. The hen will believe the box is a safe place to lay eggs because there is already an egg there!

WHAT YOU'LL NEED

Time	Difficulty	Expense
45 minutes	Moderate	$

TOOLS:

Straightedge

Permanent marker, such as a Sharpie

Vise

Jigsaw or hacksaw

Metal-cutting jigsaw blade or angle grinder

Measuring tape

Standard screwdriver

MATERIALS:

5-gal. bucket with lid

24×12×½" expanded-metal sheet

Straw

(3) 1½" wood screws

½" pipe-wrap insulation

Duct tape

HOW YOU MAKE IT

1. Remove the lid from the bucket and use the straightedge and marker to draw a cut line across the top of the lid, about 1" below center. Clamp the lid in a vise and use a jigsaw or hacksaw to cut the lid in two, along the cut line. Discard the larger piece.

2. Measure the depth of the bucket from the top edge to the bottom. Measure straight across the bucket about 2" in from the edge. Transfer these measurements to the expanded-metal sheet. Cut the sheet using the jigsaw with the metal-cutting blade or an angle grinder.

3. Secure the bucket in place to the wall of the coop, or to the supports under the bucket, by screwing it in place. Slide the cut expanded-metal sheet into the bucket pushing it against the sides to secure it. Layer 2 to 3" of straw on top of the sheet. Snap the lid in place so that the cut edge is parallel to the expanded-metal sheet.

4. Measure and cut the pipe insulation to perfectly fit the cut edge of the lid. Place the pipe insulation along the cut edge, and duct tape it in place over the bottom half of the bucket's mouth.

NESTING BOX RULES

1. NO SLEEPING ON THE JOB! Do not allow your chickens to sleep in the nesting box, because it increases the likelihood that they will defecate in the box, contaminating the eggs.

2. NO KIDS. Do not let a brooding hen raise chicks in the nesting box. The chicks will likely defecate and contaminate the box. Relocate a brooding hen to a different box or nesting area after her eggs hatch.

3. PICKUP DAILY. Harvest eggs at least once a day to protect against breakage.

4. BUILD ENOUGH HOUSING. One nesting box of the design shown here will serve three to four hens. Make sure you have enough nesting boxes for the total number of chickens.

5. COMFORT FIRST. Nesting boxes should be kept out of traffic and direct light, and should always be clean and well stocked with straw.

6. LOCK 'EM IN. Hens commonly lay early in the day, so keep them confined in the nesting box until noon.

EGG WASHER

Cleaning newly harvested chicken eggs is not just a matter of having pretty eggs to put in the refrigerator or give away to friends; it's a health issue. Egg shells are usually contaminated with dirt and chicken feces. In cooking, anything that's on the shell can possibly come into contact with the egg itself, so the shell should be clean.

Of course, cleaning each egg by hand—especially if you have a lot of laying hens—is a laborious prospect. That's why most chicken owners usually opt for some sort of automated cleaner. Any egg cleaner treads the fine line between a cleaning action that can effectively cleanse the surface of the shell and using so much force that you lose

eggs to breakage. The best way to achieve both those goals is to use air bubbles to thoroughly scrub the eggs without breaking them.

This project uses an aerator that is similar to many compressed-air designs. The beauty of it is, you don't have to own an air compressor to run this egg cleaner. It uses the exhaust port on a shop vac. Keep in mind, though, that you need to ensure that both the vacuum chamber and filter are clean before you start blowing air into the egg cleaner.

WHAT YOU'LL NEED	Time	Difficulty	Expense
	60 minutes	Moderate	$$

TOOLS:

Circular saw, jigsaw, or hacksaw

Cordless drill and bits

Clamp

Vise

MATERIALS:

½" PVC pipe (56½" [1.4 m] section)

(8) ½" PVC 45° slip elbows

½" PVC 90° slip elbow

(3) ½" PVC slip tees

½" PVC slip ball valve

5-gal. bucket

PVC primer

PVC cement

Wire egg-collecting basket

2×1½" drain and trap connector (gray coupling with hose clamps)

1×¾" adapter, Schedule 40

HOW YOU MAKE IT

1. Cut the PVC pipe into 1½" sections to connect the elbows and the ball valve, and 1" sections to connect the inline tee (adapt as necessary if your bucket is not standard size). Cut the PVC stem 20" long and the cross piece 6½" long. Dry fit the pieces and place in the bucket to ensure they will fit.

2. Assemble the aerator by coating each connection point with PVC primer. Wait 1 minute (or the manufacturer's recommended time), then apply PVC cement and slide the pieces together. Once the aerator is completed, connect the stem and ball valve in the same way. Allow the assemblies to dry.

3. Clamp the aerator ring to a work surface and drill a random series of ⅜" holes on the top and inside faces of the PVC pieces. Secure the stem in a vise and drill random holes on one side, up about 4" from where it connects to the aerator.

4. Connect a shopvac hose to the vacuum's exhaust valve, and use a hose clamp to connect the other end to the ball valve extension nipple. Use a step-up adapter, or multiple adaptors, as necessary to accommodate the vacuum hose diameter.

5. Fill the bucket half full of warm water; the top hole in the stem must be underwater. Add egg-cleaning soap, and carefully place the basket of eggs inside. Turn on the shop vac, and slowly open the ball valve until there is a healthy stream of bubbles surrounding the eggs. Let it run for 5 minutes.

6. Remove the eggs. Empty the bucket and rinse it out. Refill with warm water and replace the eggs. Rinse for an additional 5 minutes, then remove the eggs and dry them. Remove the aerator and hose it down. Empty the bucket it, rinse it out, and turn it upside down to dry.

BEE FEEDER

Bee feeders are a point of contention among beekeepers. Whether you think the bees should find their own food or not, in times of stress—when food sources are out of season, when hives are just getting established, or when there is illness present—a supplemental food source can be a boon to the hive. It may, in certain circumstances, even be crucial to the hive's survival.

The types of bee feeders available are as varied as beekeepers' opinions. There are hive feeders that actually replace a frame inside the hive, entrance feeders that attach to the entrance of the hive, hive-top feeders, and more. The feeder in this project is one of the many external feeders that are not housed inside or on the hive, but stand right next to it. Although you give up some of the protection from robbers, such as ants, that an internal feeder affords, this feeder is simpler to maintain and could not be easier to fabricate.

It feeds the bees in narrow, under-lid cavities that should present no risk of bees drowning—a key concern with any feeder. This unit works on a simple gravity system and hydrodynamics. A vacuum inside the bucket, created by the lid's seal, prevents overflow. As the bees feed and lower the level of syrup in the cavities, small holes release more syrup.

No matter what food you're putting in it, the bucket for the feeder must be clean and food grade, and have a lid with an integral gasket (to ensure an airtight seal) and a ridge below the rim that features ribs spaced regularly around the ridge. The feeder presents a tempting food source for other insects. That's why the directions include locating it in an overturned rubber or plastic garbage can lid filled with about 1/2" of water.

WHAT YOU'LL NEED

TOOLS:

Cordless drill and $\frac{3}{32}$" (2 mm) (or similar) bit

MATERIALS:

Food-grade 5-gal. bucket and tight-fitting lid (integral gasket)

Plastic or rubber garbage can lid

Time	Difficulty	Expense
20 minutes	Easy	$

HOW YOU MAKE IT

1. Remove the lid and place the bucket upside down on a work surface. Drill 2 holes in each space formed by the ribs separating the underside of the ridge.

2. Fill the bucket half full of syrup. Attach the lid and place the garbage can lid upside down next to the hive. Fill with about ½" of water. Place the feeder upside down in the center of the garbage can lid.

BEST BEE FOOD

You can't get much simpler than sugar water, but even this basic concoction spurs debate among beekeepers. Regardless of concentration, to make the sugar water (commonly known as simple syrup among bartenders and experienced beekeepers), simply combine the correct amounts of sugar and water in a large pot, bring to a simmer, and stir for 4 to 5 minutes, until the sugar completely dissolves. Allow the mixture to cool and then pour it into the feeder.

● **LIGHT CONCENTRATION.** This is made from one part sugar to two parts water. This is generally best in early spring, just as the weather starts to warm.

● **MEDIUM CONCENTRATION.** A balanced mix of one part sugar to one part water. This is a nectar-replacement food, valuable when the usual nectar sources are not producing, for whatever reason.

● **HEAVY CONCENTRATION.** This is a sugar-heavy concentration, featuring two parts sugar to one part water. This is ideal for fall or early winter in areas where plants go dormant quickly.

Do not use feeders when hive supers are in place.

CAT LITTER BOX

Even cat lovers know that a well-designed litter box is worth its weight in gold. If you have a feline friend of the indoor-cat variety, there's no getting around the fact that you need a cat litter box. The trick is to choose a box that is easy to clean, confines unpleasant smells, and takes up as little space as possible. You can find a number of models at retail, from simple rubber trays that are nothing more than containers for litter to covered bathrooms that include holders for air fresheners. But you (and your favorite kitty) will be just as well served by a thoughtfully designed, homemade five-gallon-bucket model.

The best litter box affords the animal a modicum of privacy. Cats are discreet, and they like to be out of view when doing their business. The design for this project is enclosed, which serves two purposes: the shy kitty is kept concealed during his or her "me" time, and any odors are better contained than they would be with an open, tray-type design. An enclosed structure also means that the cat can't scatter litter all over the floor or accidentally spray a nearby wall or fixture.

The number one selling point for this particular design, though, is cleanability. The half lid on the front can simply be removed to pour out dirty used litter when scoop cleaning won't do the trick, and it facilitates easy litter replacement. Not only that, but when emptied, the bucket can be sprayed out with a little dish soap and a garden hose, making it fresh as new.

TOOLS:

Measuring tape

Permanent marker, such as a Sharpie

Straightedge

Vise or clamp

Jigsaw or frameless hacksaw

Cordless drill and bits

MATERIALS:

5-gal. bucket with lid

2"×2"×5' pine (or similar)

(12) 3" flathead wood screws

½"×11" section of polyethylene self-seal pipe wrap insulation

Kitty litter

Self-adhesive furniture pads (optional)

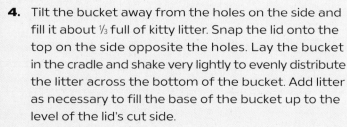

HOW YOU MAKE IT

1. Remove the lid from the bucket and measure and mark a centerline across the lid. Mark a parallel line 1" below this line—that will be the actual cut line. Clamp the lid in a vise or to a work surface, and use the jigsaw or hacksaw to cut the lid in half, along the cut line as a guide.

2. Drill several vent holes in a random pattern along one side of the bucket. This will be the top of the bucket when the bucket is lying in the cradle.

3. Build the cradle. Cut two sections of 2×2 12½" long, one section 7" long, and four sections 6" long. Assemble the cradle as shown in the illustration, drilling pilot holes and driving two 3" screws through each joint.

4. Tilt the bucket away from the holes on the side and fill it about ⅓ full of kitty litter. Snap the lid onto the top on the side opposite the holes. Lay the bucket in the cradle and shake very lightly to evenly distribute the litter across the bottom of the bucket. Add litter as necessary to fill the base of the bucket up to the level of the lid's cut side.

5. If the bucket is not firmly held by the cradle arms, stick self-adhesive felt furniture-leg pads to the arms to hold the bucket in place (a). Cut the pipe insulation to length, line the inside with a bead of silicone sealant, and secure it over the cut edge of the lid (b). Let the sealant cure before letting your cat use the litter box.

POST-MOUNTED BIRDHOUSE

If you find the idea of filling your yard with bird song attractive, you can create a home for birds to make them long-term tenants rather than short-term transients. The right birdhouse in the right place will draw in feathered friends who are nice to look at, lovely to listen to, and insect-eating machines.

Before you start building this birdhouse, you'll need to decide on what type of bird you're hoping to entice. Larger birds such as blue jays can be bullies and will take over a nest of smaller birds, if given half the chance. You'll need to figure out the proper entry hole size for the species you want to house. If the holes are too large, larger species and predators will take advantage. And, of course, if the holes are too small, the birds simply can't use the birdhouse.

Different bird species are also particular about other elements of their housing, including how close or far away the birdhouse is kept from people and how high up it will be situated. Placement is critical in any case. Birds, like other creatures, want to be safe from predators in their homes. This means keeping the birdhouse at a safe distance from bushes or other structures that cats could use as cover as they stalk their feathered prey. Make your decisions based on a "bird's-eye" view of things and you won't go wrong. Do your research and the birds you're looking for will find the home irresistible.

This project is the perfect opportunity to develop your plastic painting and stenciling skills. You can paint or decorate your birdhouse bucket with designs that help it blend in, or something more distinctive to make it a focal feature. However, it's a good idea not to attach any decoration to the bucket or post; the slick surfaces are important to help keep predators off the birdhouse and out of the birds' lives.

TOOLS:

Measuring tape

Permanent marker, such as a Sharpie

Cordless drill and bits, including 1" (25 mm) spade bit (or size that corresponds to the hole size for the birds you want to attract)

Circular saw or hacksaw

Paintbrush

MATERIALS:

5-gal. bucket with lid

PVC cement

½" PVC flange

½×6" threaded PVC nipple

3×60" PVC pipe

3" PVC slip flange

PVC primer

¾" plywood scrap at least 15" square

Sandpaper

1" flathead wood screws

Oil-based primer and paint

Quick-setting cement

(2) small metal L brackets or plastic shelf supports

3

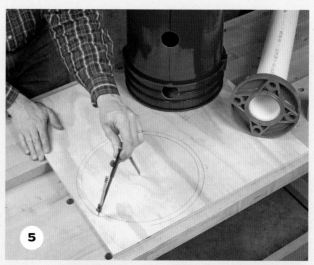

5

6

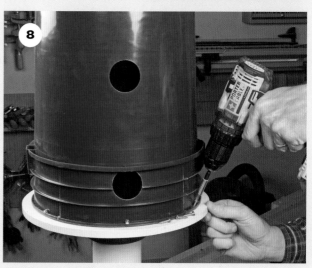

8

HOW YOU MAKE IT

1. Measure and mark two holes spaced evenly along the length of the bucket, top to bottom. Use the spade bit to drill out the holes (choose a hole size based on the size of the type of bird for which the house is meant).

2. Cut the inside of the lid out to the size that will allow it to be slid down into the bucket, as close to exactly in the middle of the bucket as possible. Test that the disc fits securely, and measure from where the disc sits to the top edge of the bucket.

3. Use PVC cement to glue a threaded ½" PVC flange to the cut disc, centered on the disc. (You can also screw the flange to the inner floor with small nuts, bolts, and fender washers for added stability, and larger bird species.) Screw a ½×6" threaded PVC nipple into the flange. Secure the disc in the bucket with the nipple sticking out of the top. Mark and cut the nipple so that the end is level with the rim of the bucket. (If the nipple is too short, use a longer nipple and cut it as necessary.)

4. Coat the end of the 3×60" PVC pipe and the inside of the 3" PVC slip flange with PVC primer. Let the primer cure according to the manufacturer's directions, and then coat the surfaces with PVC cement and attach the flange to the end of the pipe. (You can use a longer or shorter pipe, depending on how high you want the birdhouse to stand.)

5. Use the mouth of the bucket, with the cut lid rim in place, as a template to trace a circle on a piece of ¾" exterior grade plywood (or you can use hardwood if you have a large, square scrap on hand). Drill an access hole and cut around the marked circle, leaving about ½ to 1" extra all the way around. (See page 22 for instructions on cutting a circle out of plywood). Sand the plywood circle, and prime and paint with oil-based white paint, or the color you prefer.

6. Screw the plywood circle onto the post's slip flange, using the 1" screws. The flange should be centered on the circle.

7. With the divider shelf in place, place the cut lid rim on top of the bucket. Hold the post upright and plumb (you'll need a helper or a sturdy workmate for this), and sit the bucket upside down on top of the plywood circle. Make sure it is centered.

8. Drill pilot holes down through the bucket's lid rim and into the plywood. Screw the rim to the plywood with screws.

9. Dig a hole 14 to 16" deep. Pour in quick-setting cement and add water. Mix the cement with a scrap piece of wood, poking it to release any air holes. Stand the birdhouse post in the hole and check for plumb. Once you're sure that the post is plumb, screw braces of scrap wood to either side of the post and secure it in place with these temporary braces until the cement dries.

10. When the cement cures completely, decorate the pole and/or birdhouse as you desire. Fasten the L brackets or plastic shelf supports underneath the entry holes for the birds to land on. You can also drill small holes and stick short sections of dowel under the entry holes if you prefer a slightly cleaner look. Consider adding a light plastic pot with annual flowers to the top of the birdhouse so that potential predators cannot perch on top of the house.

CHAPTER 4

PLAY TIME

SOMETIMES IT'S GOT TO BE ABOUT PURE FUN!

That's why this chapter is all about indulging your inner kid (or delighting your actual kids). One of the truly awesome qualities of a plastic 5-gallon bucket is that it will put up with a ton of abuse and rambunctious recreation. That makes them absolutely perfect for play or sport structures.

Build any of the projects in this chapter and you'll be doing your family's health a favor, because all of these will get people up off the couch, out from behind screens, and doing rather than watching. They embody the best type of exercise you can get—fun and varied. Each of these will burn calories in the making and in the enjoying.

But there is a big benefit far beyond the physical reward. These projects are all a great way for the family to bond. It's like family board game night, but on steroids. You can use any of these to engage kids in a DIY ethos—have them work with you in building something they can then enjoy. It's a great way to teach building for personal payback.

So get your hardware together, gather a few basic tools, and get working on nurturing your hobbies and fun time without investing in a whole lot of new equipment.

AIR CANNON

This "weapon" is a lot safer than any toy gun you can bring in the house and, in action, seems to work like magic. An airtight membrane serves as the firing mechanism and a ball of air is the projectile. That may sound like watered-down fun at best, but the projectile carries very real force. Kids will be utterly amazed at the effects of the invisible-air "cannonball."

This is a fantastic opportunity to teach some simple science in action. The particular brand of physics that rules the movement of air is called *fluid dynamics*. The secret to an air cannon is the creation of a vortex—a swirling motion much like what you would see in water circling a drain. That action, created inside the cannon, means the air coming out of the hole carries enough energy to travel a significant distance—20 to 30 feet!

There are all kinds of fun activities to do with an air cannon. Your youngster can collect smoke from a charcoal grill or other source and blow long-traveling smoke rings (a great way to actually see the vortex action of the air out of the cannon). The blast from the cannon can extinguish candles—the safe and sane equivalent of shooting bottles with a BB gun. Left to their own devices, children of all ages will think up a wealth of fun games and uses for the air cannon, discovering more about the science of air in the process.

From there, it takes very little prompting for youngsters to make the connection between the effects of their ingenious toy and the immense power of a hurricane, tornado, or waterspout. That makes this toy one more spectacular leaping-off point for further investigation and research that could become a fascinating school science project and more.

The children can also be involved in making the air cannon, which can be done with a minimum of materials and very little expertise. None of the measurements need to be exact for the cannon to work, and your children can even customize the cannon by drawing designs on the outside.

WHAT YOU'LL NEED

	Time	Difficulty	Expense
	60 minutes	Moderate	$$

TOOLS:

Compass

Cordless drill and ⅜" (10 mm) drill bit

Permanent marker, such as a Sharpie

Tape measure

Utility knife or scissors

Straightedge

Hole punch

8" (20 cm) hole saw (optional)

Frameless hacksaw (optional)

MATERIALS:

5-gal. bucket

80-grit sandpaper

1×4" threaded PVC nipple

1" threaded PVC cap

#4 ½" flathead wood screws

6-mil plastic sheeting (clear preferable, but black will work)

Duct tape

Canopy tarp tie

HOW YOU MAKE IT

1. Use the compass to mark an 8" hole on the bottom of the bucket. Cut the hole out with a hole saw or drill a pilot hole and use a frameless hacksaw. Sand the cut edges of the hole smooth.

2. Screw the PVC cap onto the PVC nipple. Drill a pilot hole about 5" down from the top edge of the bucket. Drill a matching pilot hole in the center of the PVC cap, and then screw the bucket to the cap from the inside of the bucket, to create a handle.

3. Use the mouth of the bucket as a template to trace a circle in the middle of the plastic sheeting. Remove the bucket and measure out 4" from the circle all the way around, to trace a larger circle. Use the utility knife or scissors to cut out the larger circle. (Don't worry if the children do this part and there are small imperfections—they won't affect the performance of the completed air cannon.)

4. Fold the plastic circle in half and measure and mark the exact center along the straightedge. Use the hole punch to make a hole at this mark. (This is something that kids have plenty of experience doing, and it's a good point in the construction to get them involved.)

5. Lay a square of duct tape around the hole, to reinforce it. Feed the string end of the tarp tie through the hole until the ball end is snug against the other side. Tie a slip knot in the string of the tie, and snug it against the side opposite the ball. Cut the loop of the tarp tie, so that there are two loose ends.

6. Use a straightedge to mark two points on the bottom rim of the bucket directly across from each other. Measure up the sides of the bucket 2" from each point and make a mark. Drill ³/₈" holes at these marks.

7. Center the plastic sheeting circle over the mouth of the bucket with the ball of the tarp tie on the outside. Pull the edges of the plastic almost taut (there needs to be some play for the cannon to work), and use small strips of duct tape on four sides to hold it in place (this is much easier with a helper and a chance to make a child feel involved in the process). Lay a strip of duct tape around the edge of the plastic, all the way around, to secure it to the bucket. Make sure the duct tape has been smoothed down and is holding firmly to the bucket.

8. Pull one of the loose ends of the tarp tie through one of the holes in the bucket. Tie a knot at the end, on the outside of the bucket. Repeat with the other loose end and the other hole, and you're ready to test the cannon.

THREE QUICK AND USEFUL BUCKET OPTIONS

Family fun with buckets doesn't necessarily require involved fabrication or lots of time. Here are three that provide plenty of entertainment with minimal expense and work.

1. Popcorn Bucket

This gift container holds treats that are easy to make, but that will delight adults and children alike. Measure the inside radius at the top and bottom of the bucket and transfer those measurements to two 14" (35.6 cm) cardboard squares. Cut them into tapered rectangles, following the measurements. Cut a slot along the length of one piece from the bottom to the middle, and on the second piece from the middle to the top. Now slide the pieces together along the slots so that they form a cross. Slide this down into a clean five-gallon bucket to make four separate compartments. Decorate the bucket and fill each quarter with a different flavor of popcorn. Or substitute hard candies or other treats.

2. Beanbag Toss

Create a simple-but-engaging yard game for warm-weather fun by filling six plastic sandwich bags half full of dried beans. Wrap colored duct tape tightly around each bag. Use a hole saw to drill a hole just slightly larger than one of these beanbags in the center of a bucket's lid. Use a marker to draw a second circle around the hole in the lid, and mark the lid's rim (label with scores for the game). To play, prop up the bucket so that the top is angled toward the players. Each player gets three throws; high score wins.

3. Goal Markers

Bright bucket goal markers are perfect for quick neighborhood soccer games. Wrap blue painter's tape around a bucket in a spiral pattern and then paint the bucket in neon orange or green, or "caution" yellow. Remove the tape, turn the bucket upside down, and you have an easy-to-see marker. For a weighted marker that won't topple, fill the bucket half full of sand or dirt.

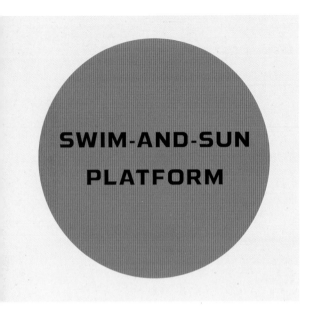

SWIM-AND-SUN PLATFORM

Water fun is multiplied with a handy platform that allows swimmers to rest between swims, provides a waterborne surface for sunbathing and diving, and can even be a floating dock where you can tie up rowboats or dinghies. This basic floating deck is all that and more. It can even be used as a crude raft on which to navigate gentle, slow-running currents.

The structure couldn't be simpler, but it does require a certain amount of careful attention to execution to ensure against any leakage. The buckets used are basically turned into bubbles of air that hold up the platform; a leak in any one of them compromises the stability of the whole platform. Keep in mind that although the buckets you use for the project can certainly be beat-up recycled units, the seal between the lid and the bucket has to be intact—the gaskets have to be undamaged. It is always smart to test the buckets by holding them upside down in a swimming pool or a bathtub full of water. After all, even a small opening or hole spells trouble over time.

One of the wonderful things about this particular project is its versatility. The basic design can be modified in any number of ways to create a larger or different shaped platform. You could use the underlying idea to create a long, thin raft or even a pontoon, outrigger-style boat. Secure it to the shore to make a short pier to which other units could be added if necessary.

One word of caution, though: Like all waterborne platforms, there is the possibility—however remote—that this one might tip and capsize in the wrong conditions and situations. The platform should never be used on the water by someone who can't swim, and don't overload the platform (no more than a couple people at any one time). If it can't handle your crowd, make a second one!

TOOLS:

Measuring tape

Carpenter's pencil

Miter saw or table saw

Cordless drill and bits

Paintbrush or roller

Tin snips

MATERIALS:

5-gal. buckets with tight-fitting lids

(2) 1½" × 3½" × 46" (3.8 × 8.9 × 116.8 cm) pine frame sides

(2) 1½" × 3½" × 23¾" (3.8 × 8.9 × 60.3 cm) pine frame ends

(1) 1½"× 3½" × 43" (3.8 × 8.9 × 109.2 cm) pine frame center beam

(10) 1½" × 3½" × 26¾" (3.8 × 8.9 × 67.9 cm) pine deck boards

3" galvanized deck screws

Waterproofing wood sealant

Perforated metal hanger strapping

1½" stainless steel washer-head screws

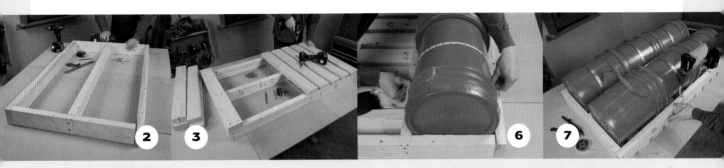

HOW YOU MAKE IT

1. Measure, mark, and cut with a miter saw or table saw all the frame pieces and deck boards from clear pine 2×4 lumber. *Note: Although you can use pressure-treated (PT) lumber to eliminate the need for waterproofing, check with local regulations to determine if PT lumber is allowed on watercraft in local waters. Many prohibit the use of PT lumber in recreational watercraft.*

2. Construct the outside frame on edge by screwing the ends to the frame sides with 3" galvanized deck screws. Measure carefully and mark the center point across each end, then line up the 2×4 center beam and screw the ends to it.

3. Lay the deck boards in place on one side of the frame, with the two end boards aligned with the ends of the frame. You can use a spacer to align the boards and create uniform spacing (the boards should be approximately 1⅜" [3.5 cm] apart). When the boards are aligned, drill pilot holes at each end and screw the deck boards to the frame with 3" galvanized deck screws.

4. Coat the entire structure with waterproofing sealant using a paintbrush or roller. Follow the instructions on the can, and apply multiple coats if recommended.

5. Flip the frame upside down so that it is resting on the deck boards. Make sure the lids are tight on all the buckets and nest three so that the bottoms sit in the lid of the bucket below. Lay the three buckets in one frame cavity. Repeat with the remaining three buckets.

6. Measure from one frame side bottom edge, over the middle of the bucket, to the frame center beam bottom edge. This will be the length of the bucket straps. Cut six bucket straps from the perforated metal hanger strapping using tin snips.

7. Position the straps and mark the screw holes (the straps on both sides will be secured by the same screw in the center beam). Drill pilot holes, then secure the straps in place with the 1½" stainless steel washer-head screws.

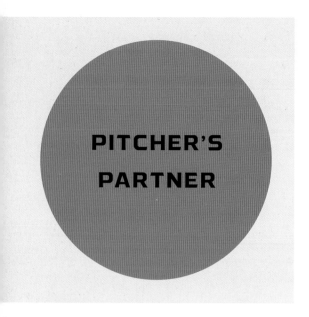

PITCHER'S PARTNER

Becoming a good—or great—pitcher is all about repetitive practice. Actually throwing the ball at a target, especially one that mimics a strike zone, is the most important workout an aspiring pitcher can get. Unfortunately for most kids, it's often hard to find a willing catcher on a regular basis. And unlike batting cages that make a solo workout easy, pitching cages are a rare commodity. The project described here is the ideal alternative to time spent throwing at a live person and an actual catcher's mitt. It's ready anytime and anyplace your junior athlete wants to put in some side work.

The construction is sized to replicate an average youth league strike zone. Make the post longer if your pitcher is a high school athlete (add 2" to 3" [5.1 to 7.6 cm]). The zone width stays the same side to side, because it equals the standard width of home plate. Although the strike zone changes with any particular batter, this zone will represent a somewhat smaller target that is perfect for helping the pitcher hone his control.

The device really earns its keep with its target elements. The red ball that hangs right in the middle of the frame represents a straight strike. The pitcher can use the black elbows as reference when he wants to throw a ball slightly outside or inside, high or low.

Ideally the pitcher should throw off a mound (or at least a raised area in the field) and try to throw a set number of pitches to different areas. The frame is especially good for alerting a pitcher if he is missing the zone on off-speed pitches such as a curveball. The unit can also be used to practice quick and accurate pick-off throws to first base, where a somewhat low throw will help the first baseman tag a straying base runner.

The bucket should be weighted down for practice sessions. This can be done with extra baseballs, nearby rocks, or anything else on hand. We've included optional instructions for making the Pitcher's Helper easier to take apart and move to and from an actual ball field, or for storage.

As with other projects, this is a good one to get your child involved with. The fabrication is not so challenging that it would overwhelm the preteen, but it involves enough measuring and exacting work to keep it interesting.

WHAT YOU'LL NEED

TOOLS:

Permanent marker, such as a Sharpie

Table saw or miter saw

Cordless drill and bits

Jigsaw or keyhole saw

MATERIALS:

1¼" × 14" (35.6 cm) PVC pipe top rail
(Schedule 40)

(2) 1¼" × 6" (15.2 cm) PVC pipe bottom
rails (Schedule 40)

(2) 2" × 18½" (47 cm) PVC pipe side
posts (Schedule 40)

2" × 16" (40.6 cm) PVC pipe main
post (Schedule 40)

80-grit sandpaper

(4) 1¼" PVC elbows (Schedule 40)

Baseball

Red spray paint

Black spray paint

1¼" PVC cap (Schedule 40)

5-gal. bucket with lid

(2) ⅜" × ¾" Phillips-head crown
bolts and nuts

PVC primer and cement

(2) 1¼" PVC tees (Schedule 40)

2" threaded eyebolt and nut

8⅛" #16 zinc-plated jack chain

Quick link

Time	Difficulty	Expense
60 minutes	Moderate	$$

HOW YOU MAKE IT

1. Carefully measure, mark, and cut the PVC pipe with a table saw or miter saw to the sizes listed on the materials list. Lightly sand the ends as necessary to ensure the cut ends slip easily into the fittings. Measure and mark the center point of the top cross brace, and drill a hole completely through the pipe at this location for the threaded eyebolt.

2. Lightly sand the elbows and the surface of one baseball. Paint the elbows black. Paint the baseball red. Let them dry completely.

3. Position the PVC cap centered in the bottom of the bucket. Drill two ⅜" (10 mm) holes on either side of the center of the cap (making sure they won't interfere with the post sliding into the cap), down through the bottom. Work on top of a sacrificial piece. Fasten the cap to the bottom of the bucket with two ⅜" × ¾" Phillips-head crown bolts and nuts.

4. Use one end of the post as a template to mark a circle in the exact center of the lid. Drill an access hole and carefully cut out the circle with a jigsaw or keyhole saw.

5. Prime and cement the main post into the cap in the bucket, securing the lid over the top of the post.

6. Lay out all the pieces for the top frame in their respective positions on a clean, flat, level work surface. Prime and cement elbows onto the ends of each side post, with the elbows facing in the same direction for each post. Cement one end of each bottom rail into one side of the tee.

7. Prime and cement one end of the top rail into one of the elbows. Cement one end of the frame bottom into the other elbow on that side (the open inlet of the tee must be pointing down, opposite the top rail).

8. Prime and cement the opposite side onto the open ends of the top and bottom at the same time. Let the frame cure completely before proceeding.

9. Fasten the threaded eyebolt and nut through the center of the top cross brace. Screw one end of the jack chain to the baseball. Attach the other end to the eyebolt with a quick link.

10. Cement the tee onto the post in the bucket, with the lid on. As an alternative, you can drive a screw through the tee and into the post, to hold the frame to the base. That way, you can unscrew the assembly if you want it to be portable. To set up the helper for use, hook the end of the chain onto the eyebolt and position the pitcher's helper 60" (1.5 m) from where the pitcher will stand.

Even with the Pitcher's Partner, the young pitcher needs to train correctly to get the most out of each workout. Pitching is a fine-motor-skill activity, and the skill needs to be developed carefully.

● Decide on a number of pitches to be thrown in any given session. To avoid injury, it's important to stick to a pitch count. Forty pitches is a good starting point, and the pitcher should divide those between different zones.

● The young pitcher should focus on developing the fastball and the changeup. Kids are enchanted with throwing a curve, but as a general rule, pitchers younger than fifteen should not attempt the pitch.

● Repetitive mechanics are key. The pitcher must develop a routine and follow it for each pitch. A good way to check mechanics is to mark the optimal landing point for the front "landing" foot. The pitcher should land in the same place every pitch.

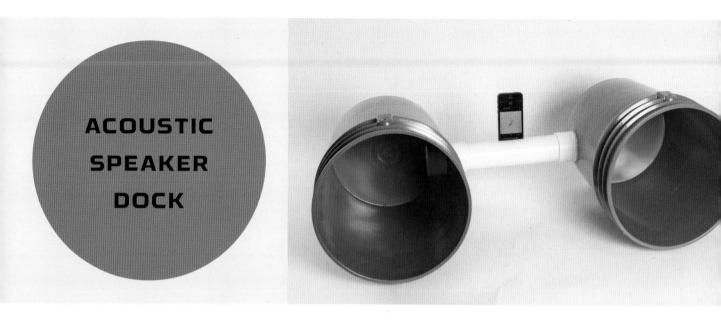

ACOUSTIC SPEAKER DOCK

Turning your cell phone or other portable music player into a mini portable stereo is simple these days. You can use one of the many self-contained portable speaker systems on the market, which let you plug and play: you simply connect the music player and presto—big sound. The downside to these systems is that they can run into the hundreds of dollars and most need their own electrical connection to operate (or else they'll burn through batteries at a fast clip). Battery-operated versions can run out of power long before your party's over. These systems can also be a little delicate—you don't want to get a lot of water, sand, or dirt on them or you'll wind up having paid a pretty penny for the equivalent of an electronic paperweight.

Fear not. Even if your budget is tight and your party will be nowhere near an electrical outlet, you can still jam the tunes using your music player. Create a much cheaper, fun, efficient, durable, and portable speaker system alternative with little more than a two five-gallon buckets, a short piece of PVC pipe, and a small bit of your time.

This speaker system is simple as can be. The secret to its success is that it exploits basic audio science. As anyone who has ever lived near a busy freeway can tell you, sound waves travel (sometimes great distances) and bounce—especially off of hard, smooth surfaces. Like the inside of a five-gallon bucket, for instance. Amplify the modest built-in speakers on your music player, and then bounce that sound all around a big echo chamber, and you've got a speaker system that does a lot with a little! It can also take a beating, so you'll never have to worry about it getting wet, or dirty, or bouncing around in the trunk of your car.

You can modify this setup to accommodate whatever music player you own. You can also jazz up your own personal five-gallon-bucket boom box with band stickers, or a marker, and some creativity. Whatever your own personal look may be, you'll control the volume of the system right from the player. Most players mount the speakers on the bottom of the unit; if your music player's speakers are on the top, you'll need to mount the player upside down in this system.

WHAT YOU'LL NEED

Time	Difficulty	Expense
45 minutes	Easy	$

TOOLS:

Vise

Measuring tape

Permanent marker, such as a Sharpie

Cordless drill and bits

2⅜" (60 mm) hole saw

MATERIALS:

2" PVC pipe (10" [25 cm] section)

(2) 5-gal. buckets

60-grit sandpaper or a fine rat-tail file

PVC cement

(2) PVC slip couplings

Silicone sealant

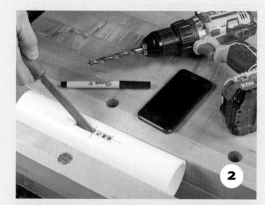

HOW YOU MAKE IT

1. Secure the PVC pipe in a vise. Measure along its length and mark the center point. Center the bottom of the music player on the center point and trace around the player's base with the marker.

2. Drill out the player's hole, using a drill bit with a diameter slightly smaller than the width of the mounting hole. Sand or file the cut edges smooth.

3. Measure and mark points 3" up from the bottom of both 5-gal. buckets. Position the end of the PVC so that the bottom edge sits on this mark, and trace around the pipe.

4. Drill out the circles with the hole saw. Dry fit the PVC pipe into one hole. The fit should be very tight. If the pipe end will not go into the hole, widen the hole a little bit at a time with sandpaper or a round file. Repeat with the second bucket.

5. Lay each bucket on its side with the holes facing each other. Stick one end of the pipe through one of the bucket holes (the player's mounting hole should be positioned straight up). Coat the pipe end with PVC cement and slide a PVC coupling onto the pipe, on the inside of the bucket. Repeat with the opposite bucket.

6. When the PVC cement is dry, lay a bead of silicone sealant around the seam where the pipe enters each bucket. Allow the sealant to dry, and then try out your new speakers.

THREE QUICK AND ENTERTAINING HALLOWEEN BUCKET OPTIONS

The 5-gallon bucket really comes into its own when holiday celebrations roll around. These projects are all about pure, silly, kid-pleasing fun. They might not be practical, but don't be surprised when the neighbors start copying your designs!

1. 5-Gallon Buck-o'-Lantern

Why kill an innocent pumpkin when you can recycle a battered old five-gallon bucket for your front porch horror show? This works best if the bucket is already orange, although it's easy enough to paint a bucket orange. Either way, draw your favorite jack-o'-lantern face on one side of the bucket. Drill pilot holes and cut out the design with a frameless hacksaw or rotary tool. Put a tea light inside, or use a more traditional candle, but be sure to put it on a saucer, to catch melting wax, and drill vent holes in the lid.

2. Small-Item Photography Light Box

Although this creation is ideal for photography of small subjects like hand-crafted jewelry you hope to sell online, it's also great to highlight a scary display for Halloween, or even a sweet diorama scene for another holiday. Cut an arched opening in the side of the bucket by first marking a 14" (35.6 cm)-wide window running up from the bottom of the bucket to a point just below the bottom flange around the top of the bucket. Complete the window shape by connecting the arc back to the bottom of the bucket. Drill an access hole and cut out the window with a jigsaw. Drill a hole in the lid for a two-piece light socket, and install the socket after connecting it to a lamp cord. To use the light box, tape white vellum paper to the inside of the bucket so that it hangs right below the lightbulb. Turn on the light and set whatever you're photographing inside.

For a different effect, swap out the white vellum for a colored sheet.

3. Candy Dumpster

Let's face it: the whole goal behind trick-or-treating is to collect as much candy as humanly possible. The weak link in the chain has always been the candy bag or the pillowcase. They just can't hold enough, so your child (or you, as the case may be) has to waste precious time heading home for a new candy carrier. Enter the candy dumpster. It has a magnificent five-gallon capacity and easy-to-use rollers that make hitting all the houses in the neighborhood before bedtime a breeze. Simply screw three to four swivel casters onto the bottom of a five-gallon bucket. If you're feeling ambitious, decorate the bucket to match your costume, and then head out to collect pounds and pounds of those free sweet treats.

BICYCLE PANNIERS

Many Americans are discovering what Europeans have known for ages: Bicycles are a superior form of transportation. Get exercise, go much faster than walking, and cover even long distances with just a little effort and no damage to the environment (or to your wallet, courtesy of a gas pump). The one big drawback to this otherwise excellent mode of transportation is the lack of onboard storage.

High-quality, roomy bicycle *panniers* (a fancy term for "saddlebags") can run more than $100, making most bike riders leery of leaving them on the bike unattended—something that is bound to be necessary in certain situations. If you're willing to go with a less polished look, you can have durable, weatherproof panniers for a few dollars or less. All you need are a couple of used 5-gallon buckets, some modest hardware, and a bike with a bike rack.

The best bike panniers have handles. That's one of the things that makes 5-gallon buckets such as a great alternative. Keep the handles on the outside when using these and they'll always be easy to remove and carry. The trickiest part of what is a basic construction process is adjusting the design for the bike rack you have. Sturdier racks include a triangular ladder design that connects the bottom of the rack to the wheel axle or frame. The main step-by-step offers a bungee cord option to secure the bottom of the bucket to this. But some racks are more basic and flimsier and may have only a single bracing post—in which case, use a longer bungee tie-down run over the top of the bike rack.

In either case, the space inside these will accommodate a fair amount of groceries, oddly shaped hardware, or other loads while protecting them as you ride. Consider painting the buckets in a style that complements your bike and reflects your own unique tastes.

WHAT YOU'LL NEED

| | **Time** 15 minutes | **Difficulty** Easy | **Expense** $$ |

TOOLS:

Permanent marker, such as a Sharpie

Cordless power drill and bits

Straightedge or level

MATERIALS:

(2) 5-gal. buckets

(2) ⁹⁄₁₆" rope loops with matching bolts and nuts

Reflective tape

(2) 12" (30.5 cm) bungee cords or tie-down straps

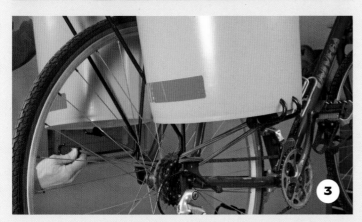

HOW YOU MAKE IT

1. Mark each bucket side for the rope loop placement. The rope loop is bolted to each bucket right under the bottom bucket flange.

2. Drill holes (a) at the marked locations using a bit that matches the size of the bolts you're using (the screws or bolts need to replace the screws provided with the rope loops). Bolt the loops in place (b).

3. Measure and mark holes perfectly opposite the rope loops and at the base of the buckets. (Use a straightedge or level to determine a straight line across the bucket from between the loop, and then perfectly vertical down the opposite bottom edge of the bucket.)

4. Drill ¼" (6 mm) holes at the marks. Apply reflective tape along what will be the back of the panniers, or use self-adhesive bike reflectors (the tape is more likely to stay in place over time).

5. Hook the rope loop over the bike rack on each side. (If you're not using an open rope loop, attach the loops to the bike rack when you attach them to the buckets in step 2.) Hook one end S hook of the bungee cord into the hole in the bottom of the bucket and stretch it underneath, hooking the other end onto a brace of the bike rack's vertical leg. Now go for ride!

MINI BASKETBALL HOOP

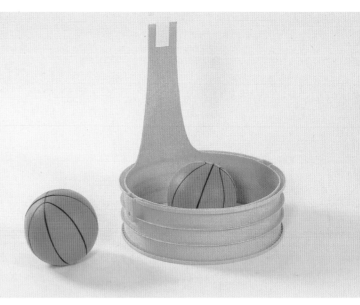

WHAT YOU'LL NEED

TOOLS:

Measuring tape

Permanent marker, such as a Sharpie

Cordless drill and bits

Jigsaw

Bar clamp

MATERIALS:

5-gal. bucket

Plastic over-the-door hook

Silicone adhesive

Flathead wood screws (optional)

Time	Difficulty	Expense
20 minutes	Easy	$

You can pack a lot of fun into a small package. This simple basketball hoop is the perfect example. It isn't right for a game of Horse in the driveway, but it is perfect for indoor full-court press with a foam or undersized toy basketball. The laughs and competition are the same as the real game.

You can use this hoop for a sporting feature by mounting it on a wall, on a door, or to any flat vertical surface to suit the situation. Just remember that even foam and toy rubber basketballs pick up a lot of dirt; you may want to put up a protective backboard of cardboard or foam core.

As fun as it can be, basketball is just one use for this handy hoop. Positioned over the laundry basket or recycling bucket, it can turn the most mundane of chores into mini bursts of fun and can ensure that kids of all ages keep their rooms (and other areas) neat and tidy. You can complete the look by adding a miniature basketball net, available at larger sporting stores and online.

HOW YOU MAKE IT

1. Remove the handle from the bucket. Mark a spine along the length of the bucket, starting 3" (7.6 cm) wide at the bottom of the bucket, and flaring to 5" to 6" (12.7 to 15.2 cm) wide at the top. The top of the spine will hold the ridged lip of the bucket that forms the actual hoop.

2. Drill an access hole and cut out the marked area with a jigsaw. Cut along the rim so that you are left with the rim attached to the flared spine. Feel free to paint or decorate the hoop in your favorite team colors.

3. To mount the hoop over a door, cut the bottom hook off a plastic over-the-door hook with a jigsaw. Use a silicone adhesive to glue the hook to the back of the spine, with the spine standing up from the hoop. Clamp it until dry. For wall or wood door mounting, drill two or three pilot holes through the spine and into a wall stud—again, with the spine above the hoop. Screw the hoop to the wall with flathead wood screws.

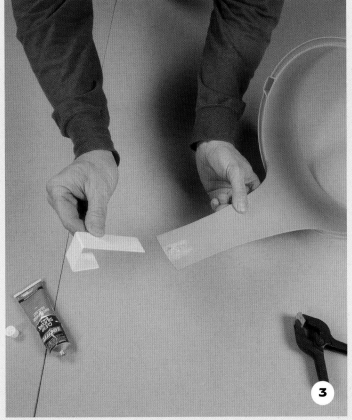

Optional: If you want a more realistic experience, add a mini backboard (12" [30.5 cm] high by 14" [35.6 cm] wide is a good size) to the hoop. Fabricate it from a scrap piece of thin plywood or even foam core. Paint a square in the center, and screw the hoop to the bottom, centered side. Screw the modified over-the-door hook described above to the back of the backboard and hang it on a bedroom door or anywhere future pro basketball stars hang out!

CHAPTER 5
BACKYARD BOUNTY

YOUR BACKYARD (OR FRONT YARD, OR EVEN SIDE YARD) PRESENTS AWESOME OPPORTUNITIES FOR GROWING PRODUCE THAT IS BETTER THAN ANYTHING YOU MIGHT FIND IN THE LOCAL GROCERY STORE, OR BEAUTIFUL FOLIAGE AND FLOWERS THAT MAKE THE SPACE A MORE DELIGHTFUL PLACE TO SPEND TIME. IN EITHER CASE, GARDENING IS MADE EASIER WITH THE HELP OF A 5-GALLON BUCKET.

That's because these buckets are constructed of exactly the type of material you need in a garden—impervious to dirt and decay. The bucket is great for keeping moisture where you need it and holding up under the extremes of weather. It doesn't hurt that buckets are also easy to fabricate, making a custom garden simple to achieve in a short amount of time.

Really, the adaptable bucket presents opportunities to garden in new and interesting ways—especially if you're dealing with the challenges of limited space. An innovative container like the **Vertical Planter** on page 116 lets you take advantage of a sun-drenched fence or even the wall of the house. The **Upside-Down Tomato Planter** on page 122 is a whole new way to grow the jewel of the summer garden.

Keep in mind that precision isn't actually key with most of these projects. Plants are going to be hiding rough cut edges and most of a bucket's surface. That doesn't mean you can't paint or stencil something like the hanging planter, but you don't actually have to worry as much about the look as you might elsewhere. The one issue that does require attention is making sure those projects where containing water is key don't leak once you've fabricated them.

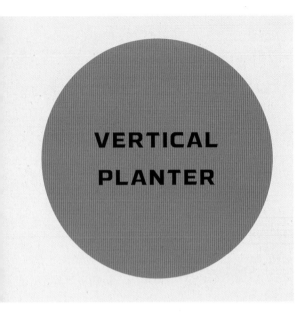

VERTICAL PLANTER

There's a reason why vertical planters remain a popular option for many homeowners: space. Whether you live in a condo with precious little outdoor area or you're a homeowner who prefers to avoid the work, expense, and maintenance of turning a large swath of your yard into a garden, space is a constant consideration for anyone looking to grow beautiful or delicious (or both) plants. This handy planter makes great use not only of the unique characteristics of a 5-gallon bucket but of all available space as well.

The planter packs a lot of growing area into fairly small dimensions. You can make and use just one of these, but because they are so easy to fabricate and cost virtually nothing, it might make more sense to craft at least two planters—using both halves of the bucket. Twin planters let you grow a double-barrel wall-mounted bounty, including both edibles and a whole planter dedicated to gorgeous flowering plants or standout foliage specimens.

Obviously certain plants will work much better in the shallow planting pockets like the cans used here. Annual herbs such as basil or chives will thrive. So will most annual flowers and any foliage plant you'd buy for a rail box. Deeper-rooted plants such as potatoes or carrots aren't good candidates. You also want to stay away from those that traditionally grow tall, like tomatoes.

There are a couple of important issues to keep in mind when using this planter. Because the cut cans are so shallow and will allow highly efficient drainage, you'll have to regularly check that your plants are getting the right amount of water. Chances are, you'll have to water them more than you would in, say, a patio pot. When mounting the planter, keep this in mind. A full load of newly moistened soil and mature plants can add up to considerable weight; make sure the structure on which you mount the planter is sturdy enough to handle the burden.

TOOLS:

Measuring tape

Permanent marker, such as a Sharpie

Straightedge or level

Handsaw

Cordless drill and bits

Jigsaw

Frameless hacksaw

Hacksaw

Tin snips

File

Wire cutters

MATERIALS:

5-gal. bucket with lid

60-grit sandpaper (optional)

Painter's tape

Recycled metal cans

½" machine screws and nuts

Potting soil

Plants

Heavy-duty zip ties

2" (5.1 cm) corner brackets (optional)

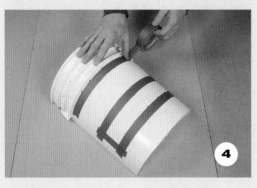

HOW YOU MAKE IT

1. Remove the bucket handle. Carefully measure and mark a cut line across the rim of the bucket. Use a straightedge or level to extend the cut line down each side of the bucket and across the center of the bottom.

2. Cut the bucket in half with the lid on, using a handsaw. *Note: You can also use a jigsaw, drilling an access hole in the bottom and cutting along the line from there. However, a jigsaw will usually be more difficult in this situation given the variations in thicknesses and the irregular surfaces.*

Optional: Make the planter more attractive by sanding off any branding or other marks on the surface. Use 60-grit sandpaper to buff the surface to a matte white or use acetone to remove any markings. Paint the surface if you prefer.

3. Remove the lid from the bucket half. Mark the plant windows by measuring 2" (5.1 cm) down from the bottom flange of the mouth of the bucket at several points along the surface of the bucket. Measure and mark several points 3" (7.6 cm) up from the bottom and 2" (5.1 cm) up from those marks. Mark 2" (5.1 cm) in from each cut edge, marking points even with the top, middle, and bottom of each window.

4. Use painter's tape to connect the three sets of marks you've made to outline the top, bottom, and sides of each planter window.

6

5. Drill access holes and cut out the top and bottom planting windows using a jigsaw or frameless hacksaw.

6. Clean and cut four recycled 15-ounce vegetable cans, 3" up from the bottom (for each window). As an alternative, you can measure and cut two 15-ounce (444 ml) and one 32-ounce (946 ml) can for a window. Use a hacksaw to make the cuts and a file to file the cut edges smooth. Drill three or four $1/16$" (2 mm) drainage holes in the bottom of each can. *Note: Cutting cans in this way can represent the potential for injury because the cut edges can be sharp. Use heavy-duty, cut-proof work gloves and exercise caution. You can also replace the cans with plastic pots (sometimes available from local nurseries for free).*

7. Drill $1/4$" (6 mm) holes at the top (under the bottom ridge), middle, and bottom of each side of the bucket, $1/2$" (1.3 cm) in from the cut edge. *Note: You don't have to drill the $1/4$" (6 mm) holes if you're attaching the planter to a solid surface such as a wood fence. See the optional step at the end for alternative mounting instructions.*

8. Starting from one side, use $1/2$" machine screws and nuts to secure the cans in place, bolting the screws from the outside into the can (two per can).

8

9. Fill the cans with potting soil and plant the plants you planned for the planter. Use heavy-duty zip ties to attach the planter to an open-weave fence through the holes you drilled in the side. Cut extra length of tongue with wire cutters.

Optional: If you're mounting the planter on a solid surface such as a wood fence, bend 2" (5.1 cm) corner brackets to an angle that better suits the surface of the bucket half. Bolt the one leg of each corner bracket to one of the $1/4$" (6 mm) holes from the inside, then screw the other leg to the fence surface so the planter is at the desired height.

THREE QUICK AND QUIRKY YARD AND GARDEN BUCKET OPTIONS

QUICK 3

Turn to the bucket for help with work chores and essential needs around the garden. A place to sit while you harvest root crops or shuck your fresh-picked corn and a quick and easy measuring device are just two of the wonderful innovations a bucket offers.

1. Graduated Cylinder

Here's an incredibly easy way to measure out amounts of water or other fluid for different purposes around the homestead—whether you're trying to water a newly planted tree with just the right amount of water or are brewing beer. Set a clean, white 5-gallon bucket on a flat, level work surface and use a gallon container, such as a plastic milk jug, to add exactly 1 gallon to the bucket. Let the water settle and mark the level with an indelible marker on two sides of the bucket. Continue adding water 1 gallon at a time and marking the levels for each. Or use a long metal yardstick held to the side of the bucket to mark inch marks and use the bucket as a rain gauge.

2. Cheap Work Stool

What gardener couldn't use a short work stool that is durable enough to hold up to the rough-and-tumble of outdoor work and cleanable as well? Look no further than a recycled 5-gallon bucket. All you'll need is some quick-setting cement, some 19" (48.3 cm) PVC pipe scraps, and about 15 minutes. Drive some spare screws through the side of the bucket, all the way around about 1" to 2" (2.5 to 5.1 cm) above the bottom. Add enough dried cement for 3" (7.6 cm) of finished cement, and add water. Poke the water and cement thoroughly with one of the pipes until the cement is a uniform texture (not too wet or too dry). Thrust the three PVC pipe scraps into the cement, equidistant around the bucket. Make sure they are flush to the inside wall surface of the bucket and then leave them to dry. When the cement is fully cured, turn the bucket over and you have a handy-dandy, knee-saving, go-anywhere work stool.

3. Lumière

Lumière is just a fancy word for a beautiful garden lantern that doesn't require electricity. Lumières are popular in gardens around the world and are often used to mark special occasions outdoors. They are usually small, but this lumière can be a wonderful centerpiece to an outdoor party. Choose a simple surface design involving small openings in the surface of the bucket—the easiest is just to drill a constellation of $1/4$" (6 mm) or smaller holes. Add about 2" to 3" (5.1 to 7.6 cm) of sand in the bucket and place a large pillar candle in the center. Light the candle for a lovely, mood-setting glow that will bring the surface design to life.

HANGING BASKET

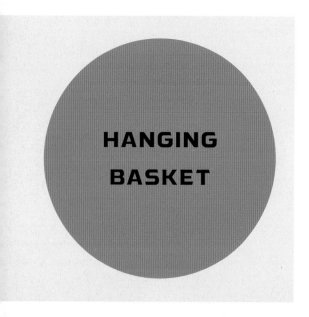

Few things are as lovely along a patio overhang or swinging from a porch rafter as a lush hanging basket. Cascading with a colorful combination of flowers and foliage, a basket like this can be a showpiece for any garden, deck, gazebo, or just about anywhere in the yard.

Hanging baskets are ideal for growing decorative plants because you completely control the culture the plants grow in. That means that you can ensure they get exactly the food and water they need—nothing more, nothing less. Also, because of the fairly modest size of any hanging basket, it won't take a ton of effort to build and plant this project, or to maintain it once it's up and growing.

Getting it "up" can be a challenge. This is a safety issue that you should take seriously. If you're not confident that the overhead support you had in mind will securely support the bucket filled with wet soil, plants, and water in the feed tube, you can either set the bucket on a wall, table, or other high surface or modify the design per the box below.

Either way, this basket was designed to hold a combination of trailing and bushy foliage and flowering specimen plants. That's not to say that you can't plant some herbs in it, but it's meant to be showy!

WHAT YOU'LL NEED

Time	Difficulty	Expense
45 minutes	Easy	$

TOOLS:

Measuring tape

Permanent marker, such as a Sharpie

Cordless drill and bits

2" (51 mm) hole saw

Hacksaw or handsaw

Vise or bar clamps

Colored pencil or chalk

Scissors

MATERIALS:

5-gal. bucket

3" × 17" (43.2 cm) PVC pipe (Schedule 40)

Landscaping fabric

(2) 3" PVC caps (Schedule 40)

PVC primer and cement

(2) ⅜" × 1" crown bolts and nuts

Potting soil

Plants

Cup hooks (optional)

Chain (optional)

HOW YOU MAKE IT

1. Measure and mark points about 3" (7.6 cm) up from the bottom of the bucket and about 6" (15.2 cm) apart around the circumference of the bucket. Repeat with a second ring of marks 3" (7.6 cm) up from the previous marks and staggered. Repeat one more time with a top ring of marks. Drill out all the holes with a 2" (51 mm) hole saw centered on each mark.

2. Measure and cut with a hacksaw or handsaw a section of 3" PVC pipe 17" (43.2 cm) long. *Note: Measure your bucket first; it should be 15" (38.1 cm) high. If it's higher, add 2" (5.1 cm) and cut the pipe to that length.* Secure the pipe in a vise or with bar clamps over a sacrificial piece and drill ⅛" (3 mm) holes all around the pipe in a random pattern.

3. Use the bottom of the bucket as a template to mark a circle on landscaping fabric with a colored pencil or chalk. Cut out the circle with scissors. Drill a random pattern of ³⁄₃₂" (2 mm) holes in the bottom of the bucket, spacing the holes about 2" (5.1 cm) apart.

4. Line the bottom of the bucket with the landscaping fabric circle. Center the 3" PVC cap upside down in the bottom of the bucket. Drill two ⅜" (10 mm) holes inside the cap, spaced as far apart as possible but positioned so that the

bolts in the holes won't interfere with the pipe slipping into the cap. Use a sacrificial piece under the bucket when you drill the holes.

5. Cut a sheet of landscaping fabric and wrap the pipe, taping it in place. Secure the cap inside the bucket with two crown bolts. Prime and cement the pipe into the cap.

6. Fill the bucket with soil to the bottom of the first holes. Tuck plants into the soil through each hole in the lowest ring.

7. Add soil to just beneath the second ring of holes and tuck plants into those holes. Repeat the process with the third (top) ring of holes, and then add soil to the top of the bucket.

8. Plant trailing or upright plants in the top of the bucket, closer than they normally would be planted. Water the soil (with the bucket over a surface that won't be damaged by any water that drains). Fill the center pipe with water and slide the second PVC cap on top.

9. Hang the basket from a sturdy overhead support or set it on a garden wall. Depending on the handle on your bucket, it may not be able to support the full weight of the bucket, wet soil, and plants. If that's the case, remove the handle and replace it with sturdy cup hooks and chain before hanging.

UPSIDE-DOWN TOMATO PLANTER

WHAT YOU'LL NEED

TOOLS:

Permanent marker, such as a Sharpie

Utility knife

Scissors

2" (51 mm) hole saw

Cordless drill and 1" spade bit

MATERIALS:

5-gal. bucket with tight-fitting lid
(preferably one with an integral gasket)

Landscaping fabric

5 gal. potting soil

Tomato plant

½" eyebolt

Chain

Gallon milk jug or plastic liter bottle

Time	Difficulty	Expense
20 minutes	Easy	$

Crazy as it might at first sound, hanging your tomato plants upside down offers a lot of benefits over planting them in the garden. Unlike in the garden, hanging locations usually have abundant direct sunlight because other garden plants aren't competing for the light and shading your tomato plants. Getting the plants up off the ground also gets them away from many diseases and pests that can decimate your delicious crop. A hanging location ensures plenty of air circulation and puts the plants right in the line of sight, where it's easy to detect any potential problems before they get out of hand.

Letting gravity sort things out also means that you don't need to provide support for the plant as it fruits—no cages or stakes. Another big plus is that you water from the top and then water and nutrients are drawn naturally down to the roots. Lastly say goodbye to weeding with an upside-down planter.

Beyond the practical, upside-down tomato plants are a visually interesting addition that—coupled with a painted and perhaps stenciled bucket—add to the look of the house or yard, wherever they're being hung.

Be aware that topsy-turvy gardening does present a few modest challenges. You have to be absolutely certain that the hook and structure from which you hang the planter can support not only the weight of the bucket when newly planted, but also the weight of a mature plant heavy with fruit and a bucketful of wet soil. Watering can also be difficult for shorter gardeners, and you should be careful to site the planter where water leaking out of the hole in the bottom isn't going to cause a problem.

That said, try this style of gardening with your tomato crop, and chances are that you'll see the opportunity for other edibles. Although you can use this planter for a variety of tomatoes, from heirloom to cherry (it is generally not appropriate for larger varieties such as beefsteak), it's also a wonderful way to grow squash, peppers, cucumbers, herbs, and even mini varieties of eggplant. In fact, you may find yourself creating an entire garden hanging from your porch rafters!

HOW YOU MAKE IT

1. Use the bottom of the bucket as a template to draw a circle with the Sharpie on the landscaping fabric. Cut out the circle with the scissors. Use the hole saw to make a 2" hole in the center of the bucket's bottom.

2. Line the bottom of the bucket with the circle of landscaping fabric. Fill the bucket with potting soil, and secure the lid in place, making sure that it's fastened tight.

3. Turn the bucket upside down and use the utility knife to slice an X in the landscape fabric covering the bottom hole. Push the root ball of the tomato plant down into the potting soil, and press firmly around the stem of the plant.

4. Screw the eyebolt into the overhang of a shed or the house, or horizontally into a fence post or other solid, secure support. Hang the bucket right-side up by its handle.

5. Cut the milk jug or liter bottle in half crosswise. Use the spade bit to make a hole in the center of the bucket lid. Push the neck of the jug down into the soil. Use the jug to add water to the plant on a regular schedule. As an alternative, run a drip irrigation line into the hole. You can also leave the bucket lid off if you prefer, and the plant may grow stems out of the top (although you risk losing dirt to wind or having animals dig in it).

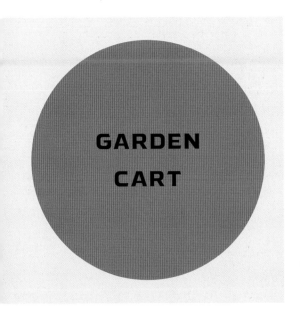

GARDEN CART

There are few tools so useful in the homeowner's yard than a portable, adaptable, rough-and-ready tote. Whether you're moving a flat of seedlings to that promising, sun-drenched flower bed or transporting a small load of river rock for the extension to your informal garden path, this study compact unit is well up to the task.

The construction will not push you to the limits of technical expertise. However, it does require attention to detail when making the measurements and subsequent cuts. All of the pieces for the base of the handle must be correctly aligned, which means they must be the right lengths. Do it correctly, though, and the handle will actually be ideal for both pushing and pulling.

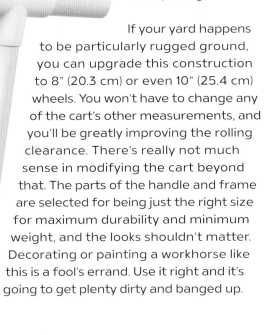

If your yard happens to be particularly rugged ground, you can upgrade this construction to 8" (20.3 cm) or even 10" (25.4 cm) wheels. You won't have to change any of the cart's other measurements, and you'll be greatly improving the rolling clearance. There's really not much sense in modifying the cart beyond that. The parts of the handle and frame are selected for being just the right size for maximum durability and minimum weight, and the looks shouldn't matter. Decorating or painting a workhorse like this is a fool's errand. Use it right and it's going to get plenty dirty and banged up.

WHAT YOU'LL NEED

	Time	Difficulty	Expense
	45 minutes	Moderate	$$

TOOLS:

Measuring tape

Straightedge

Permanent marker, such as a Sharpie

Level

Handsaw

Miter saw or hacksaw

Drill press or drilling jig

V-block

Table saw or circular saw

Power drill and bits

Wrench and Hammer

MATERIALS:

5-gal. bucket with lid

(2) 1¼" × 18" (45.7 cm) PVC pipe side rails (Schedule 40)

1¼" × 12" (30.5 cm) PVC pipe front cross brace (Schedule 40)

(2) 1¼" × 5½" (14 cm) PVC pipe handles (Schedule 40)

1¼" × 29" (73.7 cm) PVC pipe handle post (Schedule 40)

(2) 1¼" PVC tees (Schedule 40)

(2) 1¼" × 5" (12.7 cm) PVC pipe rear cross braces (Schedule 40)

(4) 1¼" PVC elbows (Schedule 40)

(2) ½" × 26" (66 cm) metal rods

Sheet of exterior-grade ½" (1.3 cm) plywood

PVC primer and cement

80-grit sandpaper

2" flathead screws

¼" × 1½" carriage bolts, washers, and nuts

(4) ⅝" washers

(4) 6" (15.2 cm) replacement wheels

(4) ⅝" hub push nuts

HOW YOU MAKE IT

1. Use a straightedge to mark a center line across the middle of the bucket lid. Measure 2" (5.1 cm) to one side of this line at several points, and mark a second straight line across the lid through these points. Use the offset line as a reference to place a level and draw lines down the side of the bucket. Connect the lines across the bottom of the bucket. Use a handsaw to cut the bucket following the offset cut line. (You'll be working with the deeper half.) *Note: You can use a jigsaw to make the cut, but it will be more difficult to control over the variations in the surface of the bucket.*

2. Measure, mark, and cut with a handsaw the frame pieces according to the measurements listed in the materials list. Precise measurements and cuts are crucial to keeping the cart's frame square. To take extra caution in this process, cut one side rail to length and use it as a template to mark the pipe for the second side rail. Cut the front cross brace first, and then stick pipe sections in either side of a tee as far as they will go, and use the front cross brace as a template to mark the cuts on the other end of the pipes for the rear cross brace sections. *Note: Depending on the type of guard and saw, your miter saw may be able to make all the cuts on the 1¼" pipe. You can also use a hacksaw to make the cuts, but make them exactly as measured.*

3. Slide an elbow onto one end of a side rail as far as it will go. Mark at the edge of the elbow (where the pipe goes into the fixture). Make a second mark ½" (1.3 cm) in from the first. Repeat this process with both ends of both side rails.

4. Use a drill press, with an elongated V-block to hold the pipe, or a drilling jig, to drill ½" (13 mm) holes directly through each end of each rail at inside end marks.

5. Dry fit the frame assembly together. Measure the diagonal measurements to ensure the frame is perfectly square. Make adjustments as necessary, reassemble the frame, and check the measurements again. Slide the metal axles through the axle holes you drilled in the side

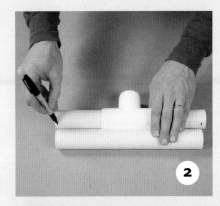

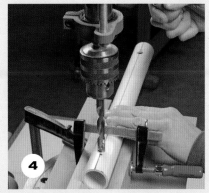

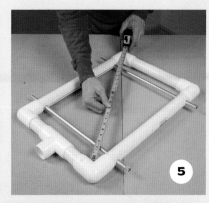

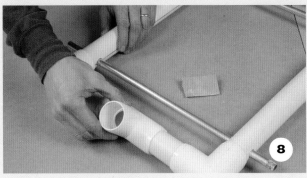

rails to ensure the holes line up. Make key marks at each joint between pipe and a fixture. Measure to be sure that the 23" × 21" (58.4 × 53.3 cm) plywood deck will sit securely across the side rails.

6. Cut the plywood deck for the cart using a table saw or a circular saw.

7. Being careful that the key marks are lined up, use PVC primer and cement to fasten the elbows onto each end of both side rails. Cement one end of the front cross brace into the keyed elbow inlet. Cement the rear cross braces into either side of a tee. Slide one side of the rear handle assembly into the side rail elbow opposite the elbow into which the front cross brace was cemented. Slide the second side rail assembly onto the front and rear cross braces.

8. Check that the handle cross braces will turn in the elbow sockets so that the handle can move (you'll need to sand the ends to allow for this). When you're satisfied that the handle assembly is able to move, remove the unattached side rail and replace it, cementing it to the front cross rail only.

9. Drill pilot holes and screw the plywood deck to each side rail, using 2" flathead screws every 3" (7.6 cm) along the edge of the deck.

10. Measure and mark the inside of the cut bucket along the bottom every 3" (7.6 cm) for the carriage bolts. Position the bucket on the frame deck, measuring to ensure it's centered all ways. Drill ¼" (6 mm) holes for the bolts, and secure the bucket to the deck with a wrench using a washer on both sides before the screw head and nut.

11. Use PVC primer and cement to fasten the handles into either side of one PVC tee. Cement the post into the central inlet. Cement the other end of the post into the cross brace tee inlet.

12. Slide the axles through the holes in the side rails. Slide a washer and a wheel onto one side of one axle. Secure the wheel in place with a hub push nut, using a hammer to tap it in. Repeat with the remaining wheels.

DRIP IRRIGATION SYSTEM

Container gardens or small backyard specimen plantings are delightful gardening options, and even more so with a "set-and-forget" watering system. What better way to create that system than by recycling the ever-handy 5-gallon bucket? This particular system is meant for areas where you placed containers or plants far from any hose bib, or where you just don't want to install a more complex, traditional drip-irrigation system.

This simple irrigation system is gravity feed, meaning that the bucket has to be physically higher than the plants it's watering. You'll find an option for a PVC cradle to achieve that for ground-level plants in the steps that follow, or you can turn to any of a number of other alternatives. Stand the bucket on a table, a garden wall, or even another 5-gallon bucket turned upside down. Elevating the bucket may also be necessary to allow clearance for the timer/controller you buy. There are lots of low-cost versions available, and most are reliable because the mechanism is so simple. Beyond that, all you'll need is simple drip line that you drape around the plants—or through the containers—you're watering. Those can be found at home centers and nurseries.

This is meant as a local system, for no more than three containers or specimen plants. It's so easy to construct that it won't take much time to make multiples for a larger area. However, if you want a streamlined option for a bigger capacity system, use a second bucket. Cut matching holes in the bottom of the new bucket and the lid of the first. Connect the holes with a two-part 4" PVC coupling and fill the top bucket with water—effectively doubling the capacity of the system.

Check the soil often in the days right after you install the system and adjust the timer controller as necessary to ensure the perfect amount of moisture is getting to the plants.

TOOLS:

Measuring tape

Permanent marker, such as a Sharpie

Power drill and bits

⅞" (22 mm) spade bit

Pliers

Miter saw or handsaw

MATERIALS:

5-gal. bucket with lid

Brass rain barrel spigot

(4) 4" × 6" (15.2 cm) PVC pipe legs (optional)

4" × 4" (10.2 cm) PVC pipe cross brace (optional)

PVC primer and cement (optional)

(2) 4" PVC tees (optional)

(4) 4" PVC caps (optional)

Drip irrigation timer/controller

Drip line

HOW YOU MAKE IT

1. Measure 2" (5.1 cm) up from the bottom of the bucket and mark for the spigot. Drill the spigot hole with a ⅞" (22 mm) spade bit (or use the bit that matches the hole for the spigot you're using—follow the manufacturer's instructions).

2. Slide the spigot post through the hole, slide the washer over the post, and tighten the spigot nut. Tighten it a quarter turn more with pliers.

3. Fill the bucket with water and check for leaks. Tighten the spigot nut if you detect any.

Optional: To assist the gravity feed action of the spigot and system, build a simple PVC pipe cradle for the bucket. Measure, mark, and cut with a miter saw or handsaw 4" PVC pipe into four 6" (15.2 cm) legs and one 4" (10.2 cm) cross brace. Use PVC primer and cement to fasten a leg into each side of a 4" PVC tee, and cement caps onto the other ends of each leg. Repeat with the remaining legs. Connect the two leg assemblies with the 4" (10.2 cm) cross brace cemented into each tee open inlet. Once the joints have cured, set the bucket on the cradle.

4. Screw the timer/controller onto the bucket spigot. Connect the drip line to the timer's pacifier end and secure it in place with the hose clamp. Open the spigot and check that there are no leaks at the connection in the system.

SCARECROW

This is a purely fun, admittedly limited-use project that will benefit most someone with a large piece of property they use to grow a bumper crop of edibles. Food is what crows are after—and why farmers build and set out scarecrows. This one can be as scary or not as you choose to make it, because *you'll* be drawing the face. You'll also be dressing it, both of which are great opportunities to get the kids involved and inspire them to exercise their unrestrained creativity while tickling the heck out of their funny bones.

The actual construction is really a skeleton. You can finish it as you see fit, including as a piece of funky art added to a wild, creative, overgrown garden design. Birds will see it as a human form, no matter how you make it look.

The construction can also be used for a pitching or quarterback target for the young athlete. Poolside, you could turn it into an attendant by draping towels over the arms and filling the bottom bucket with ice and beverages. Whatever use you put it to, you'll realize the biggest savings by recycling both the buckets for the project and the pipe. It could be left over from a home plumbing project, or you might be able to scavenge what you need from a construction site dumpster.

TOOLS:

Measuring tape

Permanent marker, such as a Sharpie

Miter saw, table saw, or handsaw

Handsaw or jigsaw

Cordless drill and bits

Level

MATERIALS:

(2) 2" × 19" (48.3 cm) PVC pipe legs (Schedule 40)

(2) 2" × 14½" (36.8 cm) PVC pipe arms (Schedule 40)

2" × 25" (63.5 cm) PVC pipe post (Schedule 40)

2" × 15" (38.1 cm) PVC pipe body (Schedule 40)

2" × 13" (33 cm) PVC pipe neck (Schedule 40)

(2) 5-gal. buckets

(6) 2" PVC caps (Schedule 40)

¼" × ¾" Phillips-head crown bolts, nuts, and lock washers

PVC primer and cement

Quick-setting concrete mix

2" PVC DWV double wye (Schedule 40)

2" PVC DWV hub double tee (Schedule 40)

Ragged old clothes, including hat

HOW YOU MAKE IT

1. Measure, mark, and cut with a miter saw, table saw, or handsaw all the 2" PVC pipe pieces to length, working on the pairs first. (Use the first of two to label the second.) Label the pipe sections to ensure you don't mistakenly cut more than you need of any individual piece.

2. Measure and mark points around one bucket, 11" (28 cm) up from the bottom. Connect the points to mark a circumference cut line, and then cut the bucket with a handsaw. You can use a jigsaw, but a handsaw is most likely going to be just as fast and easier to use.

3. Invert the two buckets, the cut over the whole bucket. Position a 2" PVC cap centered in the bottom of the uncut bucket. Drill two ⅜" (10 mm) holes on either side of the center of the cap (making sure they won't interfere with the post sliding into the cap), down through the bottoms of the buckets. Fasten the caps to the bottoms of the buckets with two ¼" × ¾" Phillips-head crown bolts and nuts.

4. Prime and cement the 25" (63.5 cm) PVC pipe post into the cap in the bottom of the uncut bucket. Cement the 13" (33 cm) PVC pipe neck into the cap in the bottom of the cut bucket.

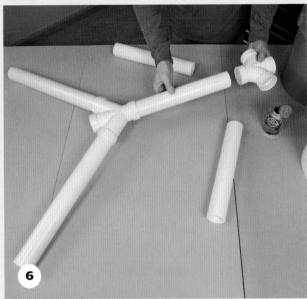

5. Pour enough quick-setting concrete mix into the uncut bucket to fill the bucket about one-third of the way with finished concrete. Add water according to the package's instructions and mix the concrete until it is the proper consistency. Check the post for plumb with a level, and screw it to a temporary brace (a scrap 2×4 will work well) laid across the top of the bucket.

6. While the concrete cures, assemble the scarecrow body. Working on a flat, level work surface, prime and cement a 19" (48.3 cm) PVC pipe leg into each angled inlet in the double wye. Cement the 15" (38.1 cm) PVC pipe body into the inlet that points away from the legs. Cement the opposite end of the body into the bottom inlet (the inlet where the two curved inlets appear to join in the fitting body) of the hub double tee. Cement the 14½" (36.8 cm) PVC pipe arms into the side inlets on the hub double tee.

7. Draw a face onto the one side of the cut bucket, which will serve as the head.

8. Prime and cement the free end of the neck into the top, open inlet of the hub double tee. Cement the cemented post into the open inlet of the double wye. Cement caps onto the ends of the arms and legs.

9. Drill a series of ¼" (6 mm) drainage holes every 2" (5.1 cm) around the bucket, right above the top of the concrete.

10. Move the scarecrow to its final location. Dress it however you want, based on old, throwaway clothes you won't mind getting wet and dirty with exposure to the elements. A long skirt that can be wrapped around the legs and pinned in place will work better than pants, which will have to be cut and glued, zip-tied, or screwed to the legs. A shirt should go on easily. Shoes and gloves can be filled out with straw or similar material and then zip-tied in place or screwed to the caps at the ends of the arms and legs. A hat and mop end screwed or glued to the top of the "head" bucket will add to the illusion.

PLANT PROTECTOR

TOOLS:

Compass or trammel

Measuring tape

Cordless drill and bits

Jigsaw or frameless hacksaw

Permanent marker, such as a Sharpie

Straightedge

Utility knife or heavy-duty scissors

MATERIALS:

5-gal. bucket

Garden insect netting

80-grit sandpaper

Silicone adhesive

Time	Difficulty	Expense
15 minutes	Easy	$

As any gardener knows, young plant seedlings are sweet temptations to a range of insects and other predators. Even deer might pull them up for a quick and handy snack, but the plant will be killed for nothing more than a taste test. Of course, creepy crawlies are not the only danger to new plants. Weather from strong winds to hail can spell death for seedlings.

Basic plant protectors are widely available at garden centers and nurseries. They come in a variety of designs, sizes, and shapes. But really, why waste the money when you can craft your own with a bare minimum of time, effort, and expertise? The size of this plant guardian is just about perfect. It will accommodate starts and plants as tall as 15" (38.1 cm) and as wide as 9" (22.9 cm).

All you need is some plastic epoxy (the best is two-in-one in a single hypodermic that mixes the two parts as you use it). Buy a quick-setting version for this project and your protector will be ready to use in a jiffy. (But avoid "instant setting" and you'll be heading off a bit of frustration!)

The simplicity of this project's design means that making multiples is super easy. Netting comes in rolls, so multiples will also be a way to amortize the cost of the netting and adhesive. That's a way to cover just about all your new plantings. And if you are the type to plant an annual flower bed, or a yearly vegetable garden, you'll be happy to know that this plant protector can be used year after year. In fact it's likely to last a decade or more, and they take up a minimum of space in storage.

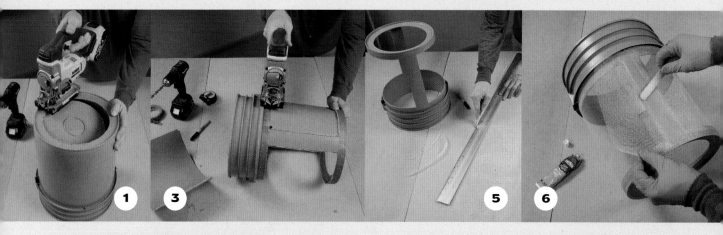

HOW YOU MAKE IT

1. Remove the bucket's handle. Use a compass or a trammel to mark a circle on the bottom of the bucket, leaving a 1" (2.5 cm) margin all around (on most buckets, this will be an 8" (20.3 cm) circle centered on the bottom). Drill an access hole and use a jigsaw or frameless hacksaw to cut out the bottom hole.

2. Measure and mark two 2" (5.1 cm) spines on opposite sides of the bucket, from the bottom of the lowest flange around the mouth, and down to the bottom. Measure and mark a 1" (2.5 cm) gluing strip at top and bottom.

3. Drill an access hole and use a jigsaw to cut from the top down to the bottom along the spines on both sides. Then cut across the bottom and top, following the marked lines, to leave the gluing strip for the netting.

4. Use this first bucket as a template to mark others if you're constructing multiples. Measure the height of the window plus the gluing strips, and the entire circumference of the bucket (the standard bucket window will be about 11" [28 cm] high and 16" [40.6 cm] wide, but check your measurements to determine exactly the height you need). The circumference will be slightly greater at the top versus the bottom, so measure both.

5. Use a straightedge and marker to transfer the measurements onto the insect netting. Cut out the netting panel with a utility knife or heavy-duty scissors. Use the bottom of the bucket as a template to mark the circular roof panel. Cut out that panel, cutting just inside the marked line.

6. Lightly sand the contact area on the gluing strips that will mate with the netting. Using a silicone adhesive meant for plastic (follow the manufacturer's instructions), lay a bead of the adhesive along the top and bottom gluing strips, and wrap the netting around bucket. Depending on what type of adhesive you're using, you may have to work quickly and in small sections. Repeat the process to glue the roof panel in place on the bottom of the bucket. *Note: Ensure the screen beds properly in the adhesive bead by using a fid, tongue depressor, or other implement to evenly spread out the adhesive once the screen is bedded along the gluing edge.*

7. Wait for the adhesive to fully cure, then set the protector over the plant and rotate the bucket back and forth a few times to secure it down into the soil. You can water the plant through the netting, without having to remove the protector.

STRAWBERRY POT

Strawberries can be a delicate fruit to grow. Susceptible to damage from snails and slugs, they can also ripen on one side if lying on the ground, and conditions have to be just right for the plants to bear the maximum amount of fruit and grow as healthy as possible.

A great way to control growing conditions and maximize the yield is to plant strawberry plants in a strawberry pot. Legend has it that the idea for this space-efficient vertical garden originated as a way to reuse broken terra cotta wine jars in ancient Greece and Italy. Whatever the origins, the idea behind a strawberry pot remains valid: grow the plants up off the ground and you make it harder for pests and diseases to ruin your crop, and easier to make sure your plants are getting everything they need to grow strong.

The pot not only allows you to control the soil and moisture your plants enjoy, but it can also regularly be turned to ensure that all the strawberry plants get the same sun exposure. One advantage to using a plastic five-gallon bucket instead of the more traditional terra cotta is that the plastic will not wick moisture out of the soil. It's also less prone to breakage than terra cotta—a big advantage if you're trying to grow strawberries in a backyard frequented by children. You can always paint it a dusty red-orange to match the look of terra cotta.

Although you may be tempted to remove the handle, it would be wise to leave it attached to the bucket. Strawberries are perennial plants; they will bear fruit for successive seasons if protected during colder months. The handle will allow you to move the bucket into a garage or storage shed after the plants are done bearing fruit, to keep them safe over the winter. It will also make it easier to turn the bucket and get even sun exposure all the way around.

Even if you're not a big fan of growing strawberries, you can use this bucket for small-space gardening. It can accommodate an herb garden or even an ornamental flower or succulent garden. The method of crafting and planting the pot stays the same.

TOOLS:

Permanent marker, such
as a Sharpie

3" (76 mm) hole saw

Cordless drill and bits

Table saw or jigsaw (or hacksaw)

Vise

Scissors

MATERIALS:

5-gal. bucket without lid

2½" PVC pipe

Landscaping fabric

Crushed gravel, broken terra-cotta,
or other coarse, irregular fill

Potting soil

Strawberry plants

Garbage-can lid

80-grit sandpaper

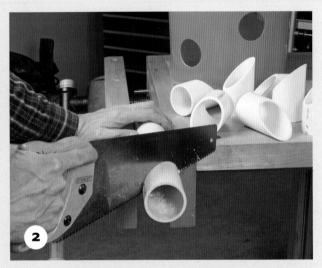

HOW YOU MAKE IT

1. Mark 3"-diameter holes around the outside of the bucket. The pattern of the holes should be staggered, with two stacked holes near the top and bottom next to a hole along the middle of the bucket. Drill out the holes with the hole saw. Turn the bucket upside down and drill a random pattern of ⁵/₃₂" holes across the bottom.

2. Cut 3" pieces of PVC pipe with the saw. The number of sections should match the number of holes you drilled in the side of the bucket. Cut the sections at a severe angle (to create the bottom of two sections), followed by a straight cut (to create the top of the next section). These are cut in the same way as if you were making stakes.

3. Cut a 16" length of the PVC pipe. Secure it in a vise and drill ¼" holes in a random pattern all around the surface of the pipe.

4. Cut a circle of landscaping fabric to fit in the bottom of the bucket. Line the bottom of the bucket with the fabric and add a 2" layer of your fill material. Stand the drilled pipe up in the center of the bucket and pour in potting soil up to the first holes.

5. Insert a pipe section into one of the lower holes at a downward angle. The long side of the point should be on the bottom. Push the pipe section in until only about 1 to $1\frac{1}{2}$" projects out from the bucket and the pointed end is secured in the potting soil. Repeat with the other lower holes.

6. Add more potting soil to fill the bucket to the top of the bottom holes. Plant the strawberry plants in these holes, firming around them with additional potting soil as necessary. Be careful to keep the crown of each plant above the level of the soil.

7. Continue this process of adding soil and planting the plants until you've filled the bucket. Plant more plants in the top as desired. Water thoroughly, in the center watering pipe and in the individual pockets. Place the bucket on the upside-down garbage can lid, on loose rock or gravel, or on bolsters so that the drain holes are not blocked.

PROJECT OPTIONS

Want a bigger haul of delicious, sweet red berries? No problem—this project is scalable. To create a bigger planter with greater yield in the same modest footprint, stack a second bucket—modified with holes and drainpipe—right over the first. Start by cutting the bottom off the top bucket. Drill the holes and stake pipes as you did for the bottom planter. Push the cut bottom edge down into the top of the bottom bucket and then plant the top bucket just as you did with the bottom. Then start enjoying all that luscious fruit.

COLD FRAME

Time	Difficulty	Expense
45 minutes	Moderate	$

Cold frames make any garden more versatile. They are the cousin to the greenhouse, offering a great deal of flexibility to the gardener. The principle behind them is to create a temporary space for tender or overwintering plants where they can be safe from freezing temperatures—and incidentally protected from predators such as insects.

Cold frames are used anywhere the temperature regularly dips into freezing temperature over the winter months. Like all cold frames, this one can be propped open to allow for venting and to prevent plants from overheating.

The structure is used for a few different purposes. It provides a great way to overwinter plants that would not survive a harsh winter in your local climate. They can be left where they are planted and protected in that space (for this use, you'll want to cut the bottom half of the bucket in half again, so that it can be pressed down into the soil around existing plantings). More often the cold frame can be used to start plants early, before the soil and air temperature warm to seasonal temperatures. You can also use a cold frame as a transitional space, to harden off seedlings that you've started inside but that may be too tender for early spring temperatures.

No matter what purpose you use it for, the plastic will help insulate against cold temperatures in both the soil and air. It is also plenty durable and can take a beating and still be useful for years to come.

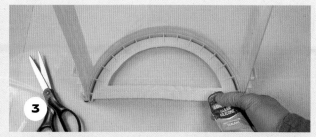

HOW YOU MAKE IT

1. Remove the bucket handle. With the lid securely attached, carefully measure and mark a cut line across the center of the lid. Use a level to extend the cut line down each side of the bucket and across the center of the bottom. Use a compass or trammel on the bottom and lid of the bucket to mark a centered circle on each. The circle should be about 9½" (24.1 cm) in diameter on the lid and about 8½" (21.6 cm) in diameter on the bottom.

2. Use a handsaw to cut the bucket in half. Use a level as a straightedge to connect the two sides of the marked arcs on the bottom and lid of one bucket half, leaving about ½" (1.3 cm) margin between the cut line and cut edge. Drill an access hole and use a jigsaw or frameless hacksaw to cut out the half circles. These will be the end windows for the cold frame.

3. Measure and mark a 10" × 16" (25.4 × 40.6 cm) window in the bucket half with the end windows, centered across the body of the bucket. *Note: A good shortcut for this is to cut out a 10" × 16" (25.4 × 40.6 cm) piece of stiff cardboard and use it as a template to mark the cutout.*

4. Drill an access hole and cut out the 10" × 16" (25.4 × 40.6 cm) window.

5. Use the bucket end windows to mark 6-mil plastic sheeting for the windowpanes. Measure and mark the plastic for the main window. Use a scissors to cut out the windows, leaving ½" (1.3 cm) extra all the way around.

6. Use plastic epoxy to glue the 6-mil plastic windowpanes in place on the inside of the bucket, covering the window openings.

7. Hold the two bucket halves together and mark one long side for the placement of the hinges. They should be centered about 6" (15.2 cm) apart. Fasten the hinge leaves to one half with the machine screws and bolts, and then to the second half.

8. Drill the hole for the stem thermometer in between two of the bucket top flanges. The stem should pass through the hole but be snug. Dig a concave hole for the bottom of the cold frame, set it into the ground, and fill the bottom half with soil, making sure the bottom half is sitting level. Plant the plants and close the top of the cold frame. Slide the thermometer in place.

MINI GREENHOUSE

A big part of the joy of being an avid gardener is the delicious anticipation of late winter and early spring. You begin to plan how your garden could look and all the wonderful things you can grow there. It's a time of renewed promise and nearly infinite possibilities.

Well, not infinite. The possibilities are usually limited not by the choices available but by expense. Plants can be pricey. Depending on the weather where you live, planting seeds may not be feasible. Your only option may be to buy flats of seedlings that have already had weeks of growing time.

You can save some of that expense and broaden the potential options for your garden by growing your own seedlings in your own custom mini greenhouse. The beauty of this creation is that, unlike even a modest backyard version, it takes up a small footprint and can be easily moved to wherever is handiest for you. It also costs just about zero dollars—money saved that can be put into your seed budget.

The idea is fairly simple: Cut windows into a 5-gallon bucket, leaving a bottom tray for soil. Use the greenhouse with an inexpensive grow light (or even a grow lightbulb in a closet flight fixture), and you control the entire environment to ensure that seedlings grow as fast as possible. The portable nature of the bucket allows you to easily position your greenhouse under whatever light source you use (and we've added a clip block for a flexible neck grow light, the kind that is widely available at home centers, nurseries, and online). It's also a boon when it comes time to take the seedlings outside so that they can be hardened off under real-weather conditions. You can take advantage of this idea by creating several greenhouses for different kinds of plants. Label the buckets so that you don't get mixed up, and you'll be able to give each type of plant its perfect growing conditions. Of course, you can also grow one stunning specimen plant from seed to a much larger size than a seedling.

	Time	Difficulty	Expense
	20 minutes	Easy	$$

TOOLS:

Measuring tape

Permanent marker, such as a Sharpie

Flexible straightedge

Cordless drill and bits

Jigsaw

Compass or trammel

Frameless hacksaw

Scissors

MATERIALS:

5-gal. bucket with two lids

6-mil plastic sheeting

Duct tape or silicone adhesive

2" deck screws

Potting soil

Seeds

Flexible stem grow light

Timer

HOW YOU MAKE IT

1. Measure and mark two 2" (5.1 cm) vertical spines on opposite sides of the bucket. The spines should run from right under the bottom ridge on the mouth of the bucket, down to 3" (7.6 cm) from the bottom. Use a flexible straightedge to draw a cut line from the bottom corner of each spine to the bottom corner of the opposite one, on each side. This will create the outline of two windows.

2. Drill an access hole and use a jigsaw to cut out the two windows, leaving the spines and bottom section. Drill a random pattern of $\frac{5}{64}$" (2 mm) drainage holes in the bottom of the bucket.

3. Use a compass or trammel to draw an 8" (20.3 cm)-diameter circle centered on the lid. Drill an access hole and use a jigsaw or frameless hacksaw to cut out the top window in the lid.

4. Use scissors to cut 6-mil plastic sheeting into panels that are $\frac{1}{2}$" (1.3 cm) larger on all four sides than the windows in the bucket. Cut the circular window for the lid 1" (2.5 cm) larger in diameter than the opening. Use duct tape or silicone adhesive to fasten each window on the inside of the bucket and underside of the lid.

5. Cut a 3" (7.6 cm) long mounting block from a 1×2 scrap. Use 2" deck screws to mount it at the top of one of the spines.

6. Fill the base with potting soil and plant the seeds you want to grow. Place the bucket in its final location on top of the second lid. Clip a flexible stem grow light to the mounting block and set a timer at the plug.

RESOURCES

Allway Tools
(718) 792-3636
allwaytools.com
Manufacturer of replacement lids for paint-filled five-gallon buckets that include a pour spout

Berkley
(800) 237-5539
www.berkley-fishing.com
Manufacturer of a fishing rod holder for five-gallon buckets

Big Bear Products
(269) 657-3550
www.bigbearproducts.com
Supplier of a five-gallon bucket lid-replacement seat, called the Silent Spin Seat

Bucket Boss
(888) 797-7855
bucketboss.com
Supplier of accessories for five-gallon buckets to be used on construction and contracting sites

Doulton Ceramic Filter Systems
(800) 664-3336
www.doulton.com
Supplier of candle-style ceramic filters for use in five-gallon-bucket filtration systems

Gamma 2
www.gamma2.net
Producer of the Gamma Seal Lid, which replaces the stock bucket lid with a tightly sealed screw-on lid

J-B Weld
(903) 885-7696
www.jbweld.com
Producer of epoxy products

Krylon
(800) 457-9566
www.krylon.com
Producer of spray paints for plastics

Oneida Air Systems
(800) 732-4065
www.oneida-air.com
Maker of the Dust Deputy, a cyclonic separator that is attached to a modified five-gallon bucket to catch dust from power tools

OrigAudio
(949) 407-6360
www.origaudio.com
Maker of a stick-on amplifier that can turn a five-gallon bucket into a music-player speaker

Original Bucket Dolly
(631) 256-5888
www.originalbucketdolly.com
Producer of a caster dolly meant for use with five-gallon buckets

Vestil Manufacturing, Inc.
(800) 348-0868
vestilmfg.com
Manufacturer of stiff plastic pail liners for five-gallon buckets

Woodcraft Supply
(800) 225-1153
www.woodcraft.com
Manufacturer of a five-gallon bucket lid replacement to convert the bucket into a shop cyclonic dust collector

ABOUT THE AUTHOR

Chris Peterson is a freelance writer and editor based in Ashland, Oregon. He has written extensively on home improvement and general reference topics, including several books in the Black & Decker Complete Guides series. His books include *Building with Secondhand Stuff: How to Re-Claim, Re-Vamp, Re-Purpose & Re-Use Salvaged & Leftover Building Materials*, *Practical Projects for Self-Sufficiency: DIY Projects to Get Your Self-Reliant Lifestyle Started*, and *Manskills: How to Avoid Embarrassing Yourself and Impress Everyone Else*. When not writing or editing, Chris spends his time hiking in the mountains of the Pacific Northwest and traveling.

INDEX